URBAN TALES OF THE BIBLE (PT.1)

BIBLE STORIES WITH A CONTEMPORARY "URBAN" FLAIR

OCTOBER 24, 2021
Written by T.S. HOLDER

Copyright @ 2021 by T.S. Holder

All rights reserved. Written permission must be secured from the publisher to use or reproduce any part of this book.

Published in Jacksonville, Fl.

The Bible stories and version used in this publication were accessed, respectively, through https://www.biblegateway.com and "Scripture taken from *The Message*. Copyright © 1993, 1994, 1995, 1996, 2000, 2001, 2002. Used by permission of NavPress Publishing Group."

Printed in the United States of America

Library of Congress Control Number: 2021924951

ISBN 9798-9854404-1-6

Website:Suprnatrl.wixsite.com/ts-holder

YouTube Channel: Outta The Cloak Room (Book Audio Excerpts)

Part One of the series explores the stories in Genesis 3 through Genesis 28 and is written for the young and old, "Church Goers" as well as the "Unchurched" that want to understand Biblical stories for themselves. It is also written for all those individuals that are crying out for Biblical knowledge from a **"relatable real life non-preachy"** source.

This book is dedicated to my spouse, who unconditionally supports me in all of my endeavors and believe me there have been many and to my mother, and my nephew who inspired me to write this.

If you have a hunger for the Word of God and want to read and understand the Word of God, this series is for you. I pray that this series helps to bring you understanding in His Word as well as assists you in developing a closer intimate relationship with Christ. Please enjoy the raw yet truthful journey that this book will take you on and remember that it is really okay to laugh.

Table of Contents

Ch. 1 – Genesis 3 - Runnin' Game in the Garden – 5

Ch. 2 – Genesis 4 - Next Gen- Cain & Abel – 12

Ch. 3 – Genesis 5 - Adam's People – 21

Ch. 4 – Genesis 6 - World Outta Control – 28

Ch. 5 - Genesis 7 - Get In The boat – 33

Ch. 6 – Genesis 8 - It's Dry Now – 38

Ch. 7 – Genesis 9 -The Rainbow, the Debriefing & Noah Gets Lit – 42

Ch. 8 – Genesis 10 - Noah's Sons Get Busy – 47

Ch. 9 – Genesis 11 - Confusion in the Camp – 51

Ch. 10 – Genesis 12 - God Spills the 411 to Abram -57

Ch. 11 – Genesis 13 - Abram & Lot Split Up – 62

Ch. 12 – Genesis 14 - Abram's got Lot's back – Lot & King K -66

Ch.13 – Genesis 15 - Abram's Vision & God's 4Ever Contract – 72

Ch. 14– Genesis 16 - The Wife & the Side Chick – 77

Ch. 15 – Genesis 17 - Abram or is it Abraham? – 83

Ch. 16 – Genesis 18 - Sarah laughs at & Lies to God – 88

Ch. 17 – Genesis 19 - A Nosey Wife & 2 "JUST NASTY" Daughters – 97

Ch. 18 – Genesis 20 - Two Time Liars – 109

Ch. 19 – Genesis 21 - Pregnant at 90/100 yr. old Huzband – 114

CH. 20 – Genesis 22 - Abraham is Acting "Suspect" – 121

Ch. 21 –Genesis 23 - Sarah Passes Away – 130

Ch. 22 – Genesis 24 - Isaac Finds a Wifey – 134

Ch. 23 – Genesis 25 - Abraham Goes Home to be with the Lord – 148

Ch. 24 – Genesis 26 - Isaac – A Liar like His Father – 156

CH. 25 – Genesis 27 - Ear Hustler Scams OG Isaac – 167

Ch. 26 – Genesis 28 - Pt 1 Finale – Ear Hustler is at it AGAIN & Jacob Leaves - 181

Chapter 1 - Genesis 3 – Runnin' game in the garden.

The serpent (Satan) was the shrewdest, coldest, and most suspect of all the untamed wild animals that YAHUAH ELOHIM created. He would swag around the Garden trying to see what he could get started. One day Satan asked the woman, "Hey girl! Hey! I know you hear me. I gotta question for you. Did Yahuah really say you must not eat the fruit from ANY of the trees in the garden?"

The woman said, "You know what, I just can't with you right now… you see me eating this piece of fruit and you gonna ask me that!! Of course we may eat fruit from the trees in the garden. Bruh, what's wrong with you? It's only THE FRUIT from the tree in the MIDDLE of the garden that we can't eat. Yah told us that we must not eat it or even touch it; cause if we do, we dead. Now I KNOW that you already know that! Boy bye!"

Satan said, "Girl You ain't gonna die! Yahuah knows that just as soon as you eat it your eyes will be wide open and you will be able to see what He can see, and you will be just like Him, knowing both good and evil. You'll know who's running a game and who's for real, who's coming for you and who's got your back."

What the serpent, Satan, said sounded real good to the woman and she bought right into that lie. Then the woman looked at the tree and said, "WOW it's beautiful and the fruit is looking so different now, it looks, it looks delish!!"

Oh girl's goal was that she wanted the wisdom that eating the fruit would give her. She said to herself, "Hmm, somebody in this camp needs some wisdom!"

So she took some of the fruit and ate it, not one piece but SOME fruit. Then she thought to herself, "What is Adam doing? He ain't doing NOTHING to get the bag!! He needs some of this too, I can't be the only one out here holding it down!"

So, she gave him some fruit and of course he ate it without even questioning where it came from. He had been eating fruit from her so long that he didn't think anything of it.

It was like immediately, that when they ate the fruit their eyes were opened, but the woman didn't think this all the way through because now both of them suddenly felt ashamed. They felt ashamed because they could now see that they were naked. Before they ate the fruit they didn't even know what naked was!

The woman said to Adam, "Dude, we gotta go shopping or something, we need to cover up."

So, they used some of the wisdom they gained from eating the fruit and sewed fig leaves together. What else were they going to find in a garden to cover up with? And so they invented the first pair of clothing by sewing some fig leaves together. A&W Clothing line was birthed!

NOW, as I said earlier, they had not thought this all the way through and did not weigh the consequences of their actions, and because of this, BUH-leeve ME, when I tell YOU, things are about to get lit!!

Later on that same day, when the cool evening breezes were blowing, and they were just chilling and thinking about what they had done earlier in the day, thinking how cool it was that they could see, and how smart they were that they created clothes to put on, they were in the moment, and oh yeah, it was all good UNTIL they heard Yahuah Elohim walking about in the garden.

"Aww snap" the woman said and told Adam, "You hear that? Is that Yah? OMG, here He comes and we know that He knows what we did, we gotta hide!"

So they tried to hide from Yahuah in the trees.

Now we all know that Yahuah already knew where they were and what they had done, but He played along with their little game of hide and seek and said to Adam, "Where are you?"

Adam said, "Uh, what had happened was I heard you walking in the garden, so I hid. I, uh, ya know, I was sceered because I was naked."

Yah said, "NAKED! Who told you that you were naked? HMM, Uh huh. Have you eaten from the tree whose fruit I commanded you not to eat? Didn't I tell your crack to stay away from THAT fruit?!!"

Here we go, it's on and poppin'!

Adam said, "Er uh, it was that woman! You know, the one that you gave me! She gave me the fruit, and I ate it. Ain't she supposed to cook and prepare the meal? I am used to eating whatever she gives me, so I didn't know what I was eating. I was hungry and didn't pay attention to what she was giving me. I had no reason not to trust her."

So, Yahuah said to the woman, "What have you done?"

The woman said, "The serpent, he's the one who deceived me and told me it was okay and he also told me I would be like you."

The woman even tried manipulating Yahuah by saying, "You know I want to be just like you, so that's why I ate it."

Since the serpent started the whole mess Yahuah said to the serpent, "Because you have started this mess, you are eternally cursed! You are cursed always, above all the animals that I made. Your mode of transportation will be by crawling on your stomach, groveling, creeping with your face down in the dust as long as you live. Yes, you will eat the dust! I'm not done with you yet, there will be hatred and hostility between you and the woman, and between your children and her children. He will hit you on your head, and you will slash his heel. That's right, right down to where your flesh is pink, "the PINK meat."

Then Yahuah said to the woman, "I will sharpen the pain of your pregnancy, and in pain you will give birth. And you will surely want to control your husband, as you did with the fruit, but he will be your master and control you."

And to the man Yahuah said, "Since you listened to your wife and ate from the wrong tree, the ground that has been so good to you and that gave you the fruit you ate, is now cursed because of you. All of your life you will struggle to scratch a living from it. You will work hard and get very little. It will grow things that you can't eat, however you will eat of its grains."

Yahuah was not finished with Adam, because He left Adam in charge of His garden.

Yahuah continued, "Until you return to the same ground that you are working, until you die, by the sweat of your brow, you are gonna have to work for it, ain't no more free rent, no more free food - you just did not know how good you had it, so by the sweat of your brow and much hard work, will you have food to eat until you return to the ground from which you were made. For you were made from dust, and when you die your body will return to dust."

Then the man, Adam, named his wife Eve, because through her all living human beings will be birthed.

And then Yahuah Elohim killed an animal and made clothing from animal skins for Adam and his wife, Eve.

Then Yahuah said to the council of heaven, "Look, the human beings know both good and evil just like we do. What if they reach out, take fruit from the tree of life, and eat it? Then they will be immortal and never die! They will live forever!"

Keep in mind, that even in the big partial lie that Satan told, he still missed his main target and got Adam and Eve to eat from the other tree, not the tree of Life.

So, YAHUAH ELOHIM threw Adam from the Garden of Eden, and sent Adam out to start working like a man. After sending him out, YAHUAH ELOHIM placed armed angels, the mighty cherubim, was on guard on the east side of the Garden of Eden. Yah placed supernatural protection to protect and guard the way to the Tree of Life by placing a flaming sword that flashed back and forth! Yahuah was serious about not letting anyone eat from the Tree of Life and becoming immortal. Adam and Eve messed it up for everyone.

You may ask, why didn't the Lord throw Eve out of the garden? Well, because Eve had to do whatever Adam said as a part of her punishment and since Adam was banished by God, Adam took Eve along with him. Oh girl didn't have a choice. I wonder if she saw this with all of the wisdom that she gained.

Side note: A Cherubim is the 2nd of the nine-fold celestial hierarchy. That hierarchy or ranking order of angels is as follows, angels, archangels, principalities, powers, virtues, dominions, thrones, cherubim and seraphim. This is a part of Christian Angelology and if you would like to know more about that you can go to en.wikipedia.org/wiki/Christian angelology.

Point to Ponder: Why did Eve so easily fall for Satan's distortion of the Truth? Was Adam working too much and not paying her enough attention? Was she just thirsty for conversation? Why did Adam not step up and be in charge of the situation and garden as the Lord had left him to do?

Take Away: Do not hide who you are, what you are doing or have done, God already knows. Instead, humble yourself before the Lord, repent and let Him cover you with His grace and love and remove the stains of your actions.

Prayer: Father we ask that You open our eyes and ears to the lies and deception of the enemy so that we are not lead into falling from the position of power that You have given us. And as You reveal things to us that we need to change, let us not stand as EVE did, in a place of manipulation, but in a place of repentance that will lead us into change.

Genesis 4: Next Gen - Cain and Abel

Since being thrown out of the garden, Adam and Eve got down to grown folks business and had sexual relations as husband and wife. Now Adam had sexual relations with his wife, Eve.

And of course, there was no birth control in those days, and anyways in Genesis 1:28 Yahuah blessed them and said, "Be fruitful and multiply, fill the earth and take it over," so, Adam and Eve took this very seriously, especially since they had messed up in the garden. So with that mission to accomplish, Eve became pregnant.

Today there is not a great need to be as fruitful and multiply. As of June 2021 the Worldometer/World Population Clock estimates that there are 7.9 billion people on this earth - so it seems that Adam and Eve accomplished their goal. When Eve gave birth to Cain, she said, "The Lord helped me to have a man child!"

Eve's statement was very powerful because there was no pain medication or epidural to soften the effects of labor so she truly walked out her punishment of sharpened labor pains.

Later Eve gave birth to another boy and named him Abel. When the boys grew up, Abel became a shepherd, while Cain worked the field. (Both worked outside in the elements – Abel was a protector of the animals (lamb, sheep, etc.), sheared the flock, milked the sheep, made cheese and overall he kept the flock in good order (sounds like a pastor to me). Cain was like a farm hand, he broke up the ground so that he could plant seeds. He had to water the vegetables, fertilize them and all things that related to farming.

Cain's job was just like what Yahuah does in us, He has to break up the things inside of us that do not please Him and plant newness and water us with His presence and His word. Cain and Abel both worked hard and had great responsibility. The products of their work was greatly needed, because they needed vegetables to go with the meat and fruits were needed for dessert and snack and to balance the meal.

When it was time for the harvest, Cain presented some of his crops as a gift to Yahuah.

Abel also brought a gift - the best lambs from the flock that had been born first. The LORD accepted Abel and his gift, but he did not accept Cain and his gift. This made Cain very angry, and he looked dejected and was feeling some kind of way.

It wasn't Cain's fault that his offering was not accepted. Many say it was his attitude or his heart as to why his offering was not accepted, I don't see any mention of that or anything that points to that in this passage. Abel's offering was accepted over Cain's offering because in Genesis 3:17 when Yahuah punished Adam for eating of the tree, he said, "Cursed is the ground."

So Cain worked the field or the ground and the ground was cursed. Yahuah does not accept cursed offerings. Also, the type of offering that Cain presented. In passages to come you will see that animals were used by the Levitical priests to atone for sin, whereas vegetables and fruits of the field were not used to atone for sin. So, while I can understand Cain's anger and feeling rejected, he just didn't know the bigger picture of why.

Cain was not around when Yahuah sentenced Adam for his part in the Garden Scandal. Cain did not know what the future held. Cain took it personal and felt that not only was his offering rejected, but he felt rejected as well. After all Cain was the first born, so he thought for sure my offering will be acceptable. Abel's offering was a lamb and scripture symbolizes Yeshua (Jesus) as the lamb, so of course Yahuah would accept the symbol of His son over crops from the field.

Yahuah said to Cain, "Why do you look so dejected, sad and depressed? Why are you acting like that? **<u>You will</u>** be accepted if you do what is right, but if you refuse to do what is right, then watch out! There will be bad and idol thoughts knocking on the door of your heart and mind, just waiting to control you and make you do something crazy. But you must not let this happen! Instead of letting sin control you, you control sin and you become sin's master."

At this point Cain could have simply asked Yahuah why was Abel's offering accepted over his offering, why was his offering so much better, but instead Cain got in his feelings and let those feelings grow and intensify. Cain felt so strongly about this, that the negative emotions (sin) started controlling his heart and thoughts towards his brother Abel.

One day Cain said to his brother Abel, "Hey Bruh, what you got going on today? Let's go out into the field and hang out for a while. Let me show you what I do every day."

And while they were in the field, Cain got the drop on Abel, attacked and killed him. Cain set his brother up and took him out. This is the first case of pre-meditated murder.

Here again we know that Yahuah knew what Cain did and what happened to Abel but afterward Yahuah asked Cain, "Where is Abel? I don't see him anywhere, where is he?"

And just as Yahuah had warned Cain that sin would control him, once again it took over and CAIN, being in his feelings, lied to Yahuah saying, "I don't know, am I my brother's keeper? I am here doing what I do, I don't have time to keep up with Abel."

Now you know that you have lost every bit of and any kind of sense that you thought you had and you know that you are under the influence of SIN when you can tell a bold face Lie to Yahuah Elohim!! SO, what I am gathering is that when Yahuah asks a question it is in our best interest to just tell the truth, because He already knows the answer. Don't be a liar like Adam and Cain and definitely don't be an Eve and use manipulation to try and get out of what you have done.

At this point, God was tired of the foolishness and got straight serious with Cain. He started squeezing the lemon and slapped Cain upside the head with the TRUTH of what he had done. Yahuah said, "What in all of heaven and earth did you do? Listen! Can't you hear it? I do! It's Abel's blood that ran in to the ground from his cold body crying out, asking me to revenge his death!"

That was to say, "Cain you killed Abel in the field that you worked and his blood went into that ground, you don't think I already know?"

God said, "Now YOU are cursed and banished from the ground, which has swallowed and soaked up your brother's blood. No longer will the ground give you good crops, no matter how hard you work! From now on you will **be a homeless wanderer, a fugitive criminal**."

Before this happened, Cain was not cursed, only his offering and the land was cursed due to his father's earlier actions, but because Cain did not do what was right, the curse is now upon him as well.

Cain spoke to the Lord out of a place of hurt and shame and said, "My punishment is too much for me! I can't handle this!! You have banished me from the land and from your presence; you have made me a homeless wanderer, a fugitive criminal. Everyone will be looking for me and anyone that runs into me while I am wandering, will kill me!"

Poor pity me. Cain needs to man up and take his punishment, but instead and once again Cain went left and took it too far, so far that he did not have the ability to overcome what came out of his mouth. Yahuah did not say that Cain was banished from His presence, but that is somehow what Cain heard. Cain's ability to take things too far left is what led Cain to kill Abel. Why was he so mad at Abel? Abel did not make Yahuah choose his offering over Cain's offering. Cain had the ability to ask Yahuah, 'what can I do so that my offering is acceptable to you?' but instead of humbling himself, he got an attitude which led him to catching a major case with Yahuah.

Missed opportunities can sometimes bring destruction to your life.

Yahuah replied, "No, now you know that I would not let that happen to you. Just remember anyone that kills you will receive a **sevenfold** punishment, a punishment that is seven times worse than what I gave you!"

Then Yahuah put a **mark** on Cain to warn anyone who might try to kill him. So on that same day Cain left the Lord's presence and settled on the east side of Eden, in the land of Nod! Cain went to the east- sy-eede!

The mark, which God placed on Cain, symbolized that Cain was under Yah's protection. It basically stated, if you touch Cain, Yahuah will deal with you and He don't play.

The text also says that Cain left the Lord's presence, not that the Lord left Cain. In Cain's mind he had only encountered the presence of the Lord in one place, he did not realize that Yahuah is omnipresent (He is always there, everywhere). How else would Yahuah know what Adam and Eve had done in the garden and that Cain had killed Abel?

Since Cain was now on the East Side of Eden, living in Nod he did not want to be alone. He had killed his brother and was banished from his hometown and everything that he knew was gone. So Cain went out and found himself a wifey, yes a BAE, and got down to grown folks business. YES, Cain had sexual relations with his wife, and she became pregnant and gave birth to Enoch.

Then Cain founded a city and named it after his son Enoch. Enoch later made Cain a grandfather and had a son named Irad. Irad made Cain a great grandfather and had a son named Mehujael. Mehujael made Cain a great-great grandfather and had a son named Methushael. Methushael made Cain a great, great, great grandfather and had a son name Lamech.

Cain thought that Yahuah had banished him from His presence, but not only was the Lord still with Cain, Cain also had favor to prosper and multiply! When Yah put his mark on Cain, that made others fear and respect him, and gave him favor in the eyes of others. It made Cain special because Yahuah's mark was upon him and this was unheard of. Also, Yah put it out there that whoever killed Cain would be punished sevenfold, meaning if you think the punishment Cain received was bad, you just touch him and see how much worse it will be for you.

Cain went on to find a wifey, have children, find and name a city after his son Enoch and his son became a big dawg. Look at what Cain and his son was able to do, because of the mark of Yahuah. Cain left a legacy to his son and even Cain's grandchildren were able to accomplish great things!

Cain's grandson Lamech was greedy and married **two** women. The first was named Adah, and the second was Zillah. Adah had a boy named Jabal, who was the first of those who raised livestock and also were tent dwellers. Jabal's brother's name was Jubal, he was amazing on the harp and flute.

Lamech's **other** wife, Zillah, had a son named Tubal-Cain. Tubal-Cain became an expert in making sturdy long lasting tools. Tubal-cain had a sister named Naamah.

One day Lamech was feeling beside himself and thought to utter these counterfeit words to his two wives, "Adah and Zillah, listen to me, you are my wives. A man attacked me, a young man, and he hurt me badly so I killed him. If someone who kills Cain is punished seven times, then the one who kills me will be punished seventy-seven times!"

Not sure who Lamech thought he was when he self-imposed a punishment on others regarding himself? Did he think he was a prophet or was he just scared and spoke to place fear in others?

Let's check in and see what Adam and Eve are up to since their son Cain was banished and Abel was killed.

Adam had sexual relations with his wife again, and she gave birth to another son. She named him Seth, for she said, "God has allowed me to have another boy to fill the void of my son Abel, who Cain killed."

When Seth grew up, he made Adam and Eve proud grandparents and had a son named Enosh.

It was at this time in history that people first began to worship the LORD <u>by name</u>. They realized how powerful the Lord's name was and began to call upon Him by name to help them in time of trouble and need and to just show Him appreciation and love.

So, Adam and Eve again fulfilled their mandate and had another child to help multiply and fill the earth.

Isn't it something that the two brothers (Cain and Seth) who had never met, both had sons and named their sons, almost identical names? Cain- Enoch and Seth –Enosh.

The plot thickens!!

Point to Ponder: Did Cain have other choices available to him, other than committing murder? Should Adam and Eve have sat their sons down and told them what they did in the garden and what the punishment was and if they had told their sons, do you think that Abel might still be alive and Cain would not be banished? OR did Adam and Eve tell their sons of their sins and only Abel listened and knew how to offer unto the Lord based on this?

Take Away: Don't let a person, event or anything push you (in your heart and mind) so far away from who you truly are that once you take actions you are unable to come back to being your true authentic self. Don't let sin rule over you.

Prayer: Father, we ask that You would show us where sin lies in our hearts and minds and what we can do that we may be an acceptable offering to You. We ask that

You would place Your mark upon us that we may find favor in Your sight and in the sight of men.

Genesis 5: Adam's People

This is the written account of the Adam's family tree. When God created human beings, he made them to be like Himself. He made them from scratch, male and female, blessed them, and called them "human." (You are Man)

When Adam was **130 years old**, he became the father of a son who was the spitting image of him. There was no need for a paternity test, because everyone could clearly see that this was Adam's son and Eve knew better than to cheat on Adam, especially after the garden incident.

Adam did not name his son Adam Junior or Adam the second, he named his son Seth. After Seth was born, **Adam lived another 800 years**, and had other sons and daughters. **Adam lived 930 years, and then he died**. Note: This is not the same Seth as the Egyptian God of Chaos.

When Seth was **105** years old, he had a son named Enosh. After Enosh, Seth lived another **807 years,** and he had other sons and daughters. Seth lived **912 years,** and then he went on to be with the Lord.

When Enosh was **90** years old, he had a son named Kenan. After Kenan, Enosh lived another **815 years**, and he had other sons and daughters. Enosh lived **905 years**, and then he went on to be with the Lord.

When Kenan was **70** years old, he had a son named Mahalalel. After the birth of Mahalalel, Kenan lived another **840 years**, and he had other sons and daughters. Kenan lived **910 years**, and then he went on to be with the Lord.

When Mahalalel was **65** years old, he had a son named Jared. After the birth of Jared, Mahalalel lived another **830** years, and he had other sons and daughters. Mahalalel lived **895 years**, and then he went on to be with the Lord.

When Jared was **162** years old, he had a son named Enoch. Jared waited a long time to have a child compared to others in his family line. I guess he wanted to be sure he was settled and had his stuff together before he brought a child into the world. After the birth of Enoch, Jared lived another **800** years, and he had other sons and daughters. Jared lived **962 years**, and then he went on to be with the Lord.

When Enoch was **65** years old, he had a son named Methuselah. After the birth of Methuselah, Enoch lived in close fellowship with God for another **300** years, and he also had other sons and daughters. Enoch lived 365 years, walking in close fellowship with God. Then one day he disappeared, because God took him! Enoch did not die, he walked on over into glory with the Lord!

When Methuselah was **187 years** old, he had a son named Lamech. After the birth of Lamech, Methuselah lived another **782 years**, and he had other sons and daughters. Methuselah lived **969 years**, and then he went on to be with the Lord.

When Lamech was **182** years old, he had a son named Noah. He named him Noah because he thought that Noah would be the one to break the family curse and they would no longer have to work hard for little and not be able to sleep because of the pain from hard work all day. He knew that the Lord had cursed the land and this is why it was so hard to work it.

After the birth of Noah, Lamech lived another **595 years,** and he had other sons and daughters. Lamech **lived 777 years**, and then he went on to be with the Lord.

After **Noah was 500 years old,** he had three sons and named them Shem, Ham, and Japheth.

The first thing that I noticed in this is that Cain is not listed at all as the son of Adam, only Seth. I also noticed that the text states that Adam had other sons and daughters but none of the other sons and daughters are mentioned by name. Don't you find this strange? It's as if Cain no longer existed. When he killed his brother and was banished, it seems that he was banished in all aspects.

This listing of Adam's family tree is actually showing us where Yeshua (Jesus) came from. Of course Yeshua could not have come from Cain or his children because Cain committed murder. Cain allowed sin to control him and his punishment of being banished was still in effect. Banishment truly meant that Cain was removed from the complete picture, even though he did thrive on the other side.

Let's briefly look at Enoch. He is not the same Enoch that Cain named a city after. This shows two sides of the coin, the good and the bad. There is a true and a counterfeit. Cain's son, Enoch, so to speak, was the counterfeit, because he did not walk with the Lord and the Lord did not take him at an early age of 365 years old. Yes, 365 years old was young back in those days.

Why did the Lord take Enoch so early? Because the Lord and Enoch were so close. Enoch did not die, there was no funeral or burial, he walked over into eternity with Yah. It is like Enoch and the Lord were in fellowship, hanging out one day and the Lord said, "Why don't you just come on into My Kingdom of Heaven and stay this time? You come each day with Me and then go back. You are in and out of the heavenly dimensions and then you go back to earth each day. You have proved yourself worthy of entrance so come on in."

The invitation was extended to Enoch and he accepted it.

Now you would think from the text that Enoch just vanished, disappeared, poof, and gone, but that is not so. In the book of Enoch (which should have been canonized meaning it should have been made an official part of the Bible) Enoch explains all that he saw, on his visits with the Lord, to his son Methuselah and he asked Methuselah to keep the writings that he had given him. So Enoch knew that he would be going to be with the Lord and was given time to not only write down what he was shown, but to explain it to his son. The Book of Enoch can be found on line in a PDF format for free.

The people that wrote Adam's family tree included Enoch because he came from one of Adam's offspring, however they left the book of Enoch out of the Bible because they could not understand what was written. They did not have the ability to understand what Enoch was passing down. Think of it this way, it was like Enoch was describing a

Maserati, Mercedes or Range Rover, ya know, something of a higher value and the people reading it only understood how to ride a camel or bicycle!! They did not have the ability to understand the deep things that Yahuah had shown Enoch and in some cases it is basically still the same way today.

Side bar: this seems to be a good place to talk about how the Bible was put together. Why do we only have 66 books in the Bible? Who decided what those 66 books would be? It is a process called Canonization (Kan-u-ni-zay-shun), which simply means that back in the day, a Council (group of men) came together to decide which writings followed a certain set of rules and standards that this council set. If the writings met the rules and standards they were included.

This came about because there were many different writings floating around that caused confusion, so the council decided that they had to set a standard. The confusion could have been that the leaders of that day did not understand the writings and thus could not explain them to the people. Often times when something is different from what is understood at that time to be normal, the different thing is discounted simply because it is outside of the existing realm of knowledge.

Now, this was all well and good at the time and it was based off of the knowledge that this council had at THAT time, however have we not now increased in knowledge and understanding? Should not the contents of the Bible be revised to include some of the books that were not understood at the time of canonization?

Also, I wanted to point out that the way the Bible is currently divided into books, chapters and verses, was later added. Originally it was not written in chapters and verses and was not titled as we see it today. Below is a chart of the divisions of the books of the Bible as they are today.

Books of the Bible

Bible - 66 Books, 1,189 Chapters 31,303 Verses

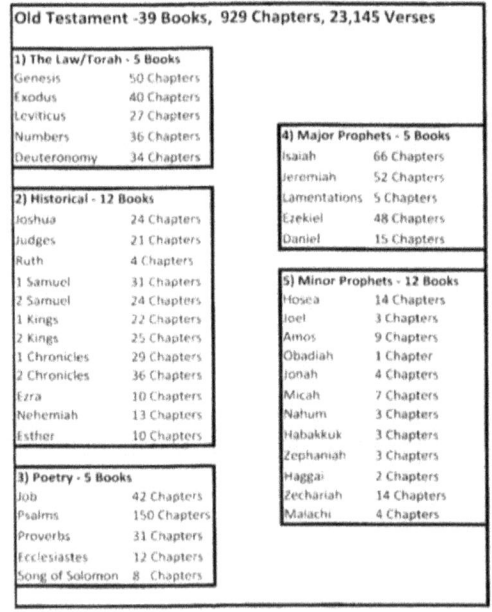
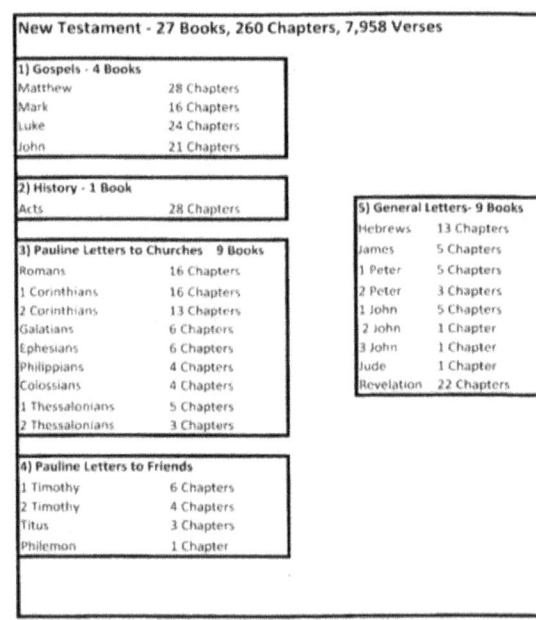

Point to Ponder: Will Noah be able to fulfill the mandate that his father Lamech placed upon him at birth to break the generational curse of working hard for a little?" What will happen if we walk in close fellowship with Yahuah as Enoch did?

Take Away: Have you ever heard or wondered where the saying, 'you are as old as Methuselah' came from? Well this is it, because he was the oldest living being in the Bible and from the line of Christ. No human lived longer than Methuselah. The only one that lived longer than Methuselah is Yahuah (God) himself, because He is everlasting.

Prayer: Lord we thank You today for a long, prosperous and healthy life just as You gave the descendants of Adam. We ask that You allow us to walk with You as Enoch did and find the fellowship with You that we need to make it in this life today.

Genesis 6: World Outta Control

Then the people began to multiply (all adults at that time were having sexual relations) on the earth, and for some reason they all had daughters!! Now when the sons of God saw how beautiful these daughters became, as they grew into women, the sons of God took anyone of them that they wanted as their wives. Then the LORD said, "My Spirit will not put up with these humans for too long a time, they are just flesh and bones. In the future, the normal human will live to be no more than 120 years."

Humans were living so long, as seen in chapter 5, that they got on Yahuah's last nerve!

In those days, and for some time after, giants lived on the earth, for whenever the sons of God had intercourse with women, they gave birth to children who became the heroes and famous warriors of ancient times.

The LORD kept noticing just how wicked humans had become, and He saw that everything they thought or imagined was, just straight up, evil. This made the Lord very sorry that He had ever made them and put them on the earth. It broke his heart in a major way.

Humans on the earth at that time were doing so many things that were evil that Yahuah's heart was broken and deeply saddened that He had created them. It's like a mother has a child, gives the child everything that they need to thrive and make a good life and the child grows into an adult and does everything that will cause them to have a troubled and dysfunctional life. The child has problems with five-0, is into drugs, commits robbery, and joins a gang. Ya know, that child has a lot of baby mama's and pays no child support. That breaks the parent's heart. The parent thinks I gave them all that I had and sacrificed so much and just look at my child acting a straight up natural fool! Did I really give birth to that, did I raise that? That's how Yahuah was feeling.

And the LORD was like, "I have had enough of this!"

And He continued, "I will wipe them all out from the face of the earth, this human race I have created. Yes, and I will destroy every living thing - all the people, the large animals, the small animals that scurry along the ground, and even the birds of the sky. I am sorry I ever made them."

However, there was one named Noah who the Lord favored. Noah was doing what he was supposed to be doing even though others were acting a straight fool, Noah did not get involved with that foolery and kept not only to himself, but his family was also on the straight and narrow.

Concerning Noah and his family. Noah was a good and decent man, the only person on earth that no one could say Noah or his family had shady dealings of any sort. They did not involve themselves with the evil they were surrounded by because Noah had a close relationship with God and did not play that. Noah had three sons named Shem, Ham, and Japheth.

In the midst of Noah and his family doing what is right, Yahuah kept seeing all of the violence and corruption on the earth. Yahuah saw that everyone on the earth was corrupt except Noah and his family.

So God made a divine executive decision and as much as it pained Him to come to this conclusion, He had to do what He had to do! He had to do what was best in His eyes. So God said to Noah, "I have decided to destroy everything that breathes! The earth is filled with violence because of THEM and it is ridiculous. M-hum, Yes, I am going to wipe everyone and everything out and start out with a fresh batch!"

And with that being said the Lord gave Noah instructions on how to build the Arc that we now know as Noah's Arc. The Lord said to Noah, "You will need Cypress wood and tar because it needs to be waterproofed inside and out. Then make decks and stalls all throughout the inside. Make the boat 450 feet long, 75 feet wide, and 45 feet high. Leave an 18-inch opening below the roof all the way around the boat. Put the door on the side, and build three decks inside the boat—lower, middle, and upper."

The Lord must have heard Noah's inner thoughts as to what was this all about and the Lord said, "Look! I am about to cover the earth with a flood that will destroy every living thing that breathes. Everything on earth will die, BUT you and I are close. You are the one person that is doing right. So I need you to build the boat and enter the boat. You and your wife and your sons and their wives will be on the boat. Bring two of every kind of animal, a male and a female, into the boat with you to keep them alive during the flood. Also, bring two of every kind of bird, and every kind of animal, and every kind of small animal that scurries along the ground, bring them with you on the boat to keep them alive. And make sure that you take enough food for your family and for all the animals."

On a side note Noah must have put plenty of roaches on the boat, cause we see plenty of them today, German roaches, water bugs, cockroaches etc. So Noah did everything exactly as God had commanded him.

Point to Ponder: With all of the evil and violence that we are seeing and hearing about on the news today is this a flashback of the days of Noah? Are we reliving what Noah and his family experienced? Is God looking upon mankind as He did in the days of Noah?

Take Away: Noah was seen by God as righteous because he was obedient to the ways of God, how does God see us today? As righteous in an unrighteous world OR does He see us as just fitting in to the ways of the unrighteous?

Prayer: Father we thank you for giving us the ability to be obedient to you even when others chose to do the opposite. We ask that You keep us in Your ways so that You will be able to see us as righteous.

Genesis 7: Get in the boat!

When Noah had done everything that the Lord told him to do, the LORD said, "Get your family, it is time to go to the boat. Only take your family and no-one else because out of all the people on earth you stand out as righteous. Remember to take seven pairs (male and female) of each animal that I told you about earlier, and that I certified as approved for eating and sacrificing to me, and take one pair of each of the others. Also, take seven pairs of every kind of bird. When I say pair, I mean male and female, this way they can breed and reproduce. Oh yeah, Noah, I need you to **make a special mental note that seven days** from now I will make it pour down rain and it will pour down rain for **forty days and forty nights**. I am doing this in order to wipe out everything that I created, that is now evil and violent, from the earth. Everything and everyone must be destroyed."

So again, Noah did everything as the LORD commanded him. Noah's wife whispered in his ear, "Honey, PLEASE make sure that we have PLEEENNNTTYY of incense, candles, perfumes and essential oils because I already know with all of those animals and birds it is going to be rankin and stankin, JUST A HOT MESS."

Noah said, "Fo sho baby girl, you know I got you."

Noah was 600 years old, but he did what the Lord said, and was on point with getting the task done like he was a youngin. It took Noah 100 years of building and gathering as the Lord said, so the people had that long to repent of their evil ways, but instead they chose to make fun of Noah and his family. Then just as God said, it started raining! The fun and games are over now!

Noah and his family got on the boat so that they would not get caught up in the flooding that was about to happen on the earth. While others laughed and called him stupid for thinking it was going to rain, for selling their house and putting all of his money into building that big awkward looking boat, Noah continued to do what the Lord commanded because he trusted in the word of the Lord and knew that it would surely happen. His wife and son's wives caught the brunt of the jokes from the ladies in the community.

The ladies would host parties and luncheons just to crack jokes about the boat and the thought of rain. One of the most popular parties was named "24/7 Rain" and everyone had to dress in wet suits, bring umbrellas and wear rain boots or shoes. However, when the rain started to fall, it wasn't so funny anymore, and it was certainly too late to get on board. After seven days of rain, the waters covered the earth and all of the haters were dead & gone.

Noah was 600 years old, on the seventeenth day of the second month, when he witnessed all the underground waters erupting from the earth, and the rain pouring down from the sky like a cat 7 hurricane. This continued for forty days and forty nights.

Shem, Ham and Japheth's wives spoke in private to their husbands and said, "Boy, ya know I really thought that your father had lost it by building this boat, rounding up the animals and saying it was going to rain, because we know that it has never rained and also with us constantly hearing the jokes of the other wives in the community we were unsure. When our backs were turned the other wives would say things like, 'Wow, if I were his wife I would have him and the whole family committed to a mental institution or even just Baker Act Noah for saying he is building the boat because the LORD told him to do so and more especially for using up all of the money we worked so hard for to build that monstrosity!'

Noah's wife and her daughter in laws were talking and said, "I sure do feel bad for Sarah and the other wives, but hey, to each his own! They told me to do me and I am so glad I did! GURL, when the Lord closed the door to this boat, I have never seen or heard anything like it before, and it was at that moment that I knew I was in the best place!"

And then in harmony, they all said together in one beat, "ON THE BOAT!"

And then they laughed out loud, while stomping their feet and slapping their hands together!

For forty days the water grew deeper and deeper, covering the ground and as the water got deeper the boat rose higher and higher above the earth so that it would float safely, even over the highest mountains. The water was more than twenty-two feet above the highest mountain peaks. And just as the Lord had said everything that was living on earth was dead, everything that breathed and lived on dry land and in the air was now dead. The haters, the pimps, the prostitutes, drug dealers, false preachers, false teachers and profits or I meant to say prophets, murderers, adulterers, child molesters, human traffickers and sex traffickers, every evil, vial, violent and corrupt thing was destroyed. God wiped them all out from the earth and the sky. Er-thing was destroyed.

If there was a radio station I am sure that "24/7 Rain" would have been at the top of the charts that day. The song would feature the animals getting on board with a major bass beat and ending with a loud symbol crash from the door of the boat closing.

Now, they were in that animal filled boat for over 150 days! That is over 5 months. Can you imagine?! Back in the day they did not have anything for sea sickness, nausea and vomiting and with all of the animal and human poo it had to be awful, but guess what, IT SURE DID BEAT BEING IN THE FLOOD!! Hey, so many complained about the 2020 COVID-19 lockdown, just imagine being on lockdown in a boat with all those animals, the noises and smells. I'd say we had it pretty good.

Point to Ponder: How was Noah and his family able to withstand all of the peer pressure and jokes from the people in the community? Would you be able to move beyond the haters and do what the Lord told you to do?

Take Away: Just as Noah and his family were preparing for what was to come and stood firm on the Word and instructions from the Lord, we need to be able to that in this day and time we are in.

Prayer: Father, we thank You for the ability to hear Your voice and instructions for our lives as we prepare ourselves each day to spend eternity with You. We ask that You would give us the strength and stamina to withstand the haters and to stay steadfast, strong and unmovable in You.

Genesis 8: It's Dry Now!

Noah and his family had been on the boat and isolated for so long, that they thought the Lord had forgotten about them, but he had not and God remembered Noah and everyone and everything that was on the boat.

God made a nice breeze to blow all over the earth, so that the floodwaters would start to leave the land and go back to the sea. The land started to dry up. The underground waters stopped flowing, the torrential rains from the sky stopped and with that the floodwaters gradually dried up. After 150 days, exactly five months from the time the rain began, the boat came to rest on the mountains of Ararat. Two and a half months later, as the waters continued to go down, other mountain peaks became visible.

After another forty days, Noah opened the window in the boat and released a raven. The raven flew all over the earth and did not stop until the land was dry. He also released a dove to see if it could find any dry ground, but the dove came right back to Noah's hand because it could find no place to land because the water still covered the ground. After waiting another seven days, Noah released the dove again. This time the dove came back in the evening hours and guess what, the dove had a fresh olive leaf in its beak and neither the dove nor the olive leaf was wet. OMG!! When they all saw that Olive leaf, chile they started shouting and cheering, because they knew it would not be long now. They knew that the floodwaters were almost gone. Noah waited another seven days and then let the dove go out again, but this time the dove did not come back. That was all they needed to know!!

Noah was now 601 years old. On the first day of the New Year, ten and a half months after the flood began, the floodwaters had almost dried up from the earth. Noah opened the door of the boat and was overjoyed because he could see that the surface of the ground was almost dry. They waited a little while longer and at last the ground was dry! That called for a celebration. Noah's wife and his daughter-in-law's were overcome with thankfulness, not just because the water was gone, but also because they were on their last little bit of incense and oils. The wives said to each other, "He may not come when you want Him, but HALLELUJAH, God was right on time! Yes, He did that!"

Then God said to Noah, "Get out of the boat, er-body out. You, your wife, your sons and daughter-in-law's. Let all the animals go so they can get down to the business of mating with each other and multiply throughout the earth."

So they all left the boat. Noah and his sons had to make sure the animals left because they had been in the boat for so long, they had captive minds. Even though the door was open, they thought they were supposed to stay.

Let the celebration begin!

Noah, being the fine craftsman that he was, drew up plans and built a legit altar to the Lord because the Lord saw that they were righteous and saved them from the flood!! He even had a place on the altar to make burnt offerings using the animals and birds that the Lord said were okay to use.

What Noah and his family did that day, sat well with the Lord and the wonderful smells from the sacrificed animals and birds made the Lord feel warm and fuzzy all over and the Lord said to himself, "I will never again do this to the human race or the earth! Yes, humans are still evil in their thoughts from birth but I will never again destroy everything. As long as the earth remains, there will be planting and harvest, cold and heat, summer and winter, day and night. The cycles of seasons and life and death will never cease to exist."

Point to Ponder: Why did the animals develop captive minds, when they had always been free to roam about before they got on the boat?

Take Away: Even though there may be a situation in your life that seems to be holding you captive just remember that it is temporary and clear your vision so that when the door of opportunity opens you are able to step through it with the boldness of knowing God did this just for you.

Prayer: Father we thank You today and ask that our vision is clear and that we are able to see the open doors that stand before us. Lord as we walk through the door(s) let us walk through with full confidence in knowing that You did this for us and that You will guide and lead us into the abundance of what that door holds for us.

Genesis 9: The Rainbow, The debriefing and Noah gets lit

If there was a radio in that day, at the top of the charts would have been "The haters are gone and we found a new home", because a new day had ARRIVED and it was A NEW BEGINNING FOR MANKIND. Then God blessed Noah and his sons and told them, "Go and do what you do, enjoy your wives. Be fruitful and multiply. Fill the earth. There is no one else on the entire earth but you, so get busy, get busy, get busy! Populate, populate, populate!"

God continued, "You are the HFIC, head family in charge. All the animals, the birds of the sky, small animals, and all the fish in the sea will fear you and you will cause them to be fearful because I have placed them in your power. I have given them to you to eat and I have given you grain and vegetables to balance out your meal. There is one thing that you must keep in mind when eating, **NEVER** eat any bloody meat. Just don't do it! It is for you own health and safety."

You see back then they did not have refrigerators, antibiotics and sanitation was not the best, so they had to be extremely cautious about what to eat. Eating the wrong things could mean a tore up stomach, sickness or even death.

Now, even though it was only Noah and his family on the earth, the Lord wanted this human race to start out right and to do what was right, so God set the laws in place, and said, "I want the blood of anyone who TAKES another person's life. If a wild animal kills a person, guess what, it must also be killed. And if someone commits the murder of a fellow human, they MUST also die. If an-y-one takes another's life that person's life must be taken by HUMAN hands. I say this because I made all human's in my image – to behave like me, to think like me, and to be compassionate and loving like me. Not to be evil, violent murderers. And besides all of that, I value what I created and you should also value each other. Now that I have given you these few simple rules go on out there and be fruitful and multiply. I expect you to repopulate this earth and have fun doing so. Go and be great!"

Then God told Noah and his sons, "Today I will set a contract with you and your people, and with all the animals that were on the boat with you—the birds, the livestock, and all the wild animals—every living creature on earth. Yes, I am confirming my contract (covenant) with you that I will never again kill all living creatures with water; never again will a flood destroy the earth."

Then God said, "I am giving you a sign of my contract (covenant) with you and with all living creatures, for ALL future generations. I am placing MY rainbow in the clouds. It is the sign of my contract with you and with all the earth. When you see clouds cover the earth, look for the rainbow in the clouds, this will again remind you and Me of the contract where I have said I will not ever again destroy the inhabitants of the earth with a flood. This is an eternal contract and the rainbow will continuously exist to remind Me, you and future generations."

In reading this passage it begs me to say that I am unsure of why there is such a big ta-do over the LGBTQ community using the rainbow as their symbol. Did not God say this was a contract with ALL people for ALL generations?! Sometimes people want to be so profound that they totally miss the relevant point. God said the rainbow was for all people for all generations. Reading really is fundamental!

The sons of Noah who came out of the boat with their father were Shem, Ham, and Japheth. (Ham is the father of Canaan.) From these three sons of Noah came all the people who now populate the earth.

After the flood, Noah began to cultivate the ground, and he planted a vineyard and had a wine cellar. Noah missed his wine because he drank the last of it on the boat so he had to get his wine cellar back in order. One day Noah drank too much, got drunk and passed out naked in his tent. Oh my, my, my! Ham, the father of Canaan, saw that his father was naked and went outside and blasted his father's business to his brothers. He thought that it was too funny because he had never seen his father this way before. Back in the old country, Noah had a man cave and could go in there and no one would see him. However, when Ham saw this, the one thing he missed was giving his father respect and privacy. Why couldn't Ham have just covered his father and went on about his business? But NO he had to put his father on blast and yell out to his brothers, "Yo dude come and look at dad, man I ain't never seen him like this before. Oh boy done got drunk and naked!"

Ham did not realize the pressure that his father had been under in preparing the boat, getting the animals, the food and putting up with the naysayers and haters. That trip in the boat really did put a toll on him, it was not a cruise to the Caribbean.

When Shem and Japheth realized what Ham was saying they took a robe, held it over their shoulders, and backed into the tent to cover their father. As they did this, they looked the other way so they would not see him naked. They respected and honored their father in this manner. They had compassion and understanding, they would not want to be put on blast if this was them, and so they did what they would expect others to do for them if they were in this situation.

When Noah finally woke up from being passed out drunk, he learned just how his younger son, Ham, acted and what Ham said when he was drunk and naked. Noah was embarrassed and 38 hot. He was so pissed that Ham, HIS OWN SON, had come for him. Noah was so livid that he cursed Canaan, the son of Ham! He cursed his grandson that wasn't even born yet!! Now you know Noah was in his feelings, because grandparents always spoil their grandchildren, not curse them!!

Noah said, "May Canaan be cursed! That's right I said it. May he be the lowest of servants to his relatives."

Noah said this because Ham's actions were the lowest of the lowest. Then Noah blessed his son Shem, and made Canaan his grandson, Shem's servant! As for Japheth, Noah asked God to give him more land and greater influence and to also be prosperous as his brother Shem and guess what? You are right, Noah also made Canaan Japheth's servant.

Noah lived another 350 years to ripe old age of 950, and then he went on home to be with the Lord.

Point to Ponder: Why did Ham find it so amusing that his father was drunk and naked? Was he that immature?

Take Away: When we find ourselves in a situation to honor and cover someone who has found themselves overwhelmed by life circumstances, let us remember that if it was not for the grace of God, it could have been us. And in remembering this, let us reach out to assist that person and not "situation" shame them.

Prayer: Father we thank You for giving us a compassionate heart and mind towards others that struggle and are overwhelmed with what life has thrown their way. We ask that You give us the ability and means to help this person and because we choose to help instead of situation shame we ask that You bless them even more.

Genesis 10: Noah's sons get busy!

Noah's sons, Shem, Ham and Japheth, were very serious about populating and replenishing the earth and many children were born to them after they got off that boat. Greatness was in their loins!

Japheth had 7 children named Gomer, Magog, Madai, Javan, Tubal, Meshech, and Tiras.

His 1st born child, Gomer, had three children named Ashkenaz, Riphath, and Togarmah. His 4th child named Javan, had four children named Elishah, Tarshish, Kittim, and Rodanim, and their children were people of the sea that did a lot of traveling and had their own language, clan and identity. They were individuals who stepped outside of the box, did their own thing and made their own way. They were not held back by boundaries.

The youngest son of Noah, Ham, you know the one who put his father Noah on blast for being drunk and naked, had four children; Cush, Mizraim, Put, and Canaan. Cush had five children and name them Seba, Havilah, Sabtah, Raamah, and Sabteca. Raamah Had two children named Sheba and Dedan.

Cush was also the ancestor of Nimrod, who was the first heroic warrior on earth. Since he was the greatest hunter in the world, his reputation went before him. Everyone knew of him. People would give him his props by saying, "This man is like Nimrod, the greatest hunter in the world."

Cush built his kingdom in the land of Babylonia, with the cities of Babylon, Erech, Akkad, and Calneh. From there he expanded his territory to Assyria, building the cities of Nineveh, Rehoboth-ir, Calah, and Resen (the great city located between Nineveh and Calah).

Mizraim was related to the Ludites, Anamites, Lehabites, Naphtuhites, Pathrusites, Casluhites, and the Caphtorites, from whom the Philistines came. The Philistines are very famous in chapters ahead because this is Goliath the giant's people. You know Goliath, the one that David KO'd in the first round!

Canaan's oldest son was Sidon, the ancestor of the Sidonians. Canaan was also the grandson that Noah cursed way before he was even born, and he was an ancestor of the Hittites, Jebusites, Amorites, girgashites, Hivites, Arkites, Sinites, Arvadites, Zemarites, and Hamathites. WOW, to be cursed by his grandfather, Canaan's seed did a lot of populating! The Canaanite clans eventually spread out, and the territory of Canaan extended from Sidon in the north to Gerar and Gaza in the south, and east as far as Sodom, Gomorrah, Admah, and Zeboiim, near Lasha. Those were the descendants of Ham.

Now don't sell Shem short because he is mentioned last. Chile, Shem had many Sons and was the ancestor of all the people of Eber. Shem's sons were Elam, Asshur, Arphaxad, Lud, and Aram. The people of Aram were Uz, Hul, Gether, and Mash.

Arphaxad was the father of Shelah, and Shelah was the father of Eber. Eber had two sons. The first was named Peleg (which means "division"), because while he was living, the world was divided into different language groups.

Eber's brother's name was Joktan. Joktan was the ancestor of Almodad, Sheleph, Hazarmaveth, Jerah, Hadoram, Uzal, Diklah, Obal, Abimael, Sheba, Ophir, Havilah, and Jobab. All these were descendants of Joktan. The territory they occupied extended from Mesha all the way to Sephar in the eastern mountains. These were the descendants of Shem.

These are the people that came from Noah's sons being fruitful and multiplying the earth. After the flood, all the nations of the earth came from them taking their assignment to get busy, get busy, get busy and populate, populate, populate very serious.

Point to Ponder: This is the second time that we have seen someone who has been cursed be fruitful, multiply and increase. The first was Cain and now Canaan. Does this show that even though a person is cursed God is still with them and loves them? Does it show that God still wants the best for all of his children or that after God blesses them Satan steps in, takes over and increases them, but does the increase last and amount to what God would have done for them?

Take Away: What we have read is about legacy and generations and how Noah set his son's up for generational wealth and increase and how Noah's sons passed that down to their children and the blessing continued throughout their family line. Now the question is, are we setting our children up for generational increase and success, if not, why? It is never too late to start.

Prayer: Father we thank you for giving us the wisdom and knowledge to increase and to set up generational wealth and increase for generations to come. We ask for strategies, witty inventions and all of the necessary funds and skills that would not only set us up for wealth, but that would also set up wealth for generations to come.

Genesis 11: Confusion in the Camp

At one time in history all the people of the world talked the same, used the same words and everyone could understand everyone, regardless of what country or tribe they were from. It was not like it is today with all the different languages, slang and urban tones, however when the people started moving to the east, they found some prime land in Babylonia and decided to stay there.

The people decided that they wanted to make this a permanent place to stay and held a meeting to make further plans. At the meeting the question was asked: "What y'all think about making hard bricks with fire?"

At that time in history and in this particular part of the world bricks were used instead of stone, and tar was used for mortar (cement) to build houses and buildings.

At the meeting everyone agreed that this is how they would build the city, out of brick and tar. Then they all joined in and decided to build a great city and add a tower that would reach the sky. They thought that this tower would make them famous and keep them together. This would be a city unlike any other city at that time. They would no longer be wandering all over the earth, but this would give them the ability to all stay in one place.

We learned from Adam and Eve in the garden and from Cain trying to hide the fact that he committed murder that the Lord already knew what was in the crevices of their heart.

The Lord decided He would check them out and see what they were up to and when He did He said, "OMG!! Look! These people are really united, and they all speak the same language. With all of them working together there is nothing that they cannot do, nothing is impossible for them to do!"

So the Lord spoke with the Counsel of heaven and said, "Come, let's go down there and throw some confusion in the mix and make them speak different languages. This way they won't be able to understand each other and can no longer build the tower."

You see the people were trying to reach heaven with the tower. So, when confusion arrived, the unity and brotherhood of the people was broken up and the people were scattered all over the world, and of course the great plans they had for the brick and tar city and the tower was scattered with them. After the confusion hit, the people sounded as if they were a babbling brook saying, "blah, blah, blah."

And that is why and how the city was named Babel, because that is where the LORD confused the people with different languages. When the Lord did this they all went their separate ways. What else could they do, they could no longer understand each other.

Can you imagine, talking to your friends one day and having great plans to do something the next day; going to sleep being all anxious to wake up and get started on the project the next day, all kinds of ideas to put down and make it happen AND THEN you finally wake up and you can't understand a word that anyone is saying. Can you imagine what that looked like and how they felt?

This may seem cruel and mean of the Lord, but He knew that if the tower was built the people would only occupy one portion of this big earth that He had given them and with the unity they had among themselves, they would soon consider themselves gods because there would be nothing that they could not do working together as one.

Let's change the focus a little bit and get back to Noah and his family.

In the previous chapter we looked at Noah's family tree, so right now we are going to drill in on Shem's family and this will show how Abram (Abraham) came about. The story of Abraham is in chapter 12, but this will lay the foundation.

Two years after the great flood and two years after the boat landed Shem was **100** years old and at 100 years of age he had a son named Arphaxad. After Arphaxad, Shem lived another **500** years, to the age of 600 and inside of those many years he had other sons and daughters.

WOW, children at 100 and beyond, these were some blessed people. However, after Shem, they started having children at an age much like the people of our time and they did not live as long as the people of Adam and Eve's day. Remember in Genesis 6:3 the Lord said, "My Spirit will not put up with these humans for too long a time, they are just flesh and bones. In the future, the normal human will live to be no more than 120 years."

Well, this starts the shift in age, five chapters later, the lifespan starts to decrease.

When Arphaxad was **35** years old, he had Shelah. After Shelah, Arphaxad lived another **403 years** and yes of course, he had other sons and daughters.

When Shelah was **30** years old, he had Eber. After Eber, Shelah lived another **403 years** and most certainly had other sons and daughters.

When Eber was **34** years old, he had Peleg. After Peleg, Eber lived another **430 years** and had many other sons and daughters.

When Peleg was **30** years old, he had Reu. After Reu, Peleg lived another **209 years** and had a lot of other sons and daughters.

When Reu was **32** years old, he had Serug. After Serug, Reu lived another **207 years** and it goes without saying that Reu had other sons and daughters.

When Serug was **30** years old, he had Nahor. After Nahor, Serug lived another **200 years** and in those 200 years he populated the earth with many other sons and daughters.

When Nahor was **29** years old, he had Terah. After Terah, Nahor lived another **119 years** and felt the need to continue the mandate of multiply the earth, so he had other sons and daughters.

Well there it is, Genesis 6:3 in full view!

When Terah was **70** years old, he had three sons named Abram, Nahor, and Haran.

Now that we have established what Noah's sons and grandsons were doing let's dig a little deeper.

At 70 years old Terah had three sons, Abram, Nahor, and Haran. Haran made Terah a grandfather and had a son named Lot. Sadly enough after Haran had Lot he went on home to be with the Lord while he was still in the place named the Ur of the Chaldeans, his hometown. This was hard on his father Terah, because he had to bury his son, which seemed so out of order.

Meanwhile, Abram and Nahor found them a wifey. The name of Abram's bae was Sarai, and the name of Nahor's bae was Milcah. Milcah and her sister Iscah were daughters of Nahor's brother Haran who died early in age. Gone but not forgotten.

Now even though Abram and Sarai were getting busy on a regular basis, Sarai was unable to become pregnant and at this point had no children. This was unusual since everyone was being fruitful and multiplying. Sarai probably felt like an outcast and the other woman surely spoke cruel of her, to her face and more especially behind her back. The cruel women said things like, "She can't have children, hmmm! Well I say that there must be some hidden sin in her life or her family line. And anyways where did Abram find her? Yes, she is pretty and all but if you can't give a man a child, beauty don't matter much! He could have had someone else, like me! Yes, he could have had all of THIS, but naw, he had to choose her! Uh, huh, that's what he gets."

One day Terah took his son Abram, his daughter-in-law Sarai (his son Abram's wife), and his grandson Lot (his deceased son Haran's child) and moved them away from

Ur of the Chaldeans. They left their hometown to find better and to get away from those gossiping women. They headed for the land of Canaan, but they stopped at Harran and decided to stay there a while. While they were there Terah lived for another 205 years and went on home to be with the Lord.

Points to Ponder: Why is it that only Nahor and Abram are mentioned as finding a wife? Could it be because they will have a child that will become great in the eyes of God and man? Do you think that Terah took his son (Abram) and daughter-in-law (Sarai) away from their hometown because they talked so badly about Sarai not being able to have children? Do you think that the negative words of the naysayers could have caused Sarai not to have a child? Why would he move away from his hometown, his friends and all of his family?

Take Away: When we are surrounded by negativity, negative words, or in a negative atmosphere with negative people this can have a polarizing and negative impact on what we are trying to accomplish in life. This negativity can cause you to lose focus and never reach your goals or destiny. When there is negativity, cut it at the root and move away from it. Do not allow negative people or any form of negativity to keep you from your life's destiny and goals. Let the haters go!

Prayer: Lord we thank You today for giving us the boldness to let the haters go and for the strength to move forward into our destiny and accomplish the goals that You have for our lives.

Genesis 12: God Spills The 411 to Abram

After Terah passed away, the LORD spoke to Abram and said, "It's time for you to leave this country. Leave this place where your father brought you to. Leave all your friends and relatives and relocate to a place that I will show you."

The Lord spoke further and said, "If you are obedient and do what I am instructing you to do, I will make you into a powerful nation and bless you and make you famous. You will have so much that you will be able to help others and give to others. Now, because you are so special to Me, remember that whoever is down with you, I will be down with them and by the same token if someone comes for you I will come for them. Ev-u-re-baw-dy on the earth will receive coins, a bag and a blessing, because of you."

This sounds like the time to be obedient especially with all of the promises of greatness and blessings. Abram could see the 4K HD picture the Lord was painting for him and stepped on out on what the Lord said to him. So, at the age of 75, Abram picked up his things and got out of the city of Haran as the LORD had instructed him to do.

Abram and Lot were day ones, thier relationship went way back, so Lot went with him and of course Abram took his BAE, Sarai. Abram was a wealthy man, some called him bouche and others called him bou-ghetty. This is why the women in his hometown were in an uproar about who he married. They were looking for a young handsome "rich" man, but I am pretty sure that Abram saw how thirsty they were and chose Sarai, whose name literally means princess.

Abram took all of his possessions with him, his money, his animals, and all of the people that worked for him. Abram set his GPS and started out towards a place called Canaan. Remember Canaan, the grandson of Noah, the one that Noah cursed because of Ham blasting his drunken, nakedness? Well, this is his land.

Months later, they arrived in Canaan, but Abram kept going until he reached Shechem (means shoulder) and set up camp near the oak of Moreh (means teacher, fruitful) in the land of the Canaanites. Abram was leaning on the Lord's shoulder to teach him and make him even more fruitful.

Then the LORD appeared to Abram and said, "I will give this land to your children."

So Abram built an altar, just like Noah did, and dedicated it to the LORD, who had appeared to him. Abram built that altar because he wanted to always remember that this is the place the Lord appeared to me and gave this land to my children and children's children, to my family line.

After that, Abram traveled south and set up camp in the hill country where Bethel (means a holy place) was on the west and Ai (means Ruins or heap) was on the east. There he built another altar, right in the middle of a place of blessing and a place of ruins, and dedicated it to the LORD, and he worshiped the LORD. Then Abram continued traveling south, stopping here and stopping there, going toward the Negev (means dry).

Abram's plans were put on hold because a severe food shortage happened suddenly in the land of Canaan, so Abram had to re-route and go down to Egypt, where he lived as a foreigner. The closer he came to Egypt the more anxious he became. He was actually down right scared, because he knew the type of people that lived in Egypt were nothing to play with!! Man they were wicked and oppressive, they thought that they were IT and since he was an outsider he expected trouble.

Abram must have forgotten who sent him on this journey. Whenever the Lord sends you some place believe me He has taken into account everything that will happen. We may not know what will happen on a detour, just as Abram didn't, but God does and He has our back.

As Abram was approaching the border of Egypt, Abram said to his wife, Sarai, "Hey BAE! Girl you know that you are a gorgeous chocolate woman. MM, hmmm!! When the Egyptians see you, they will say, 'Man, look at shorty, she is beautiful. Let's kill him,` then we can have her!' So, baby PLEASE tell them you are my sister. Then I won't be killed and I will be accepted and honored, because they are trying to get with you."

Looks to me like Abram recognized the gift and queen that he had by his side!

And sure enough, it happened just as Abram said when they got to Egypt. Man, ev- uh-ree-one started awwing and oohing at how beautiful Sarai was. It was like she was on parade in a beauty pageant. But yo, when she arrived at the palace and the heads in charge saw her, they sang like they were in church, singing Sarai's praises to Pharaoh, their king.

Now, because of her beauty and how she captured everyone's eye Sarai was taken into the palace. And again as Abram thought it would happen, Pharaoh gave Abram many gifts because of Sarai. Pharaoh gave him sheep, goats, cattle, male and female donkeys, male and female servants, and camels. He loaded Abram up because of Sarai's beauty.

But, Abram should have known that the lie would have consequences!! He didn't think about that. Now the LORD sent terrible plagues on Pharaoh and everyone connected to him! Why? Because of Abram's lie and Pharaoh having Sarai in his house when Sarai should have been with her husband Abram! Sarai was the gift, the woman that the Lord had given to Abram for his wife and she was not to be shared or passed around. Sarai should not have been with Pharaoh.

When the plagues hit, Pharaoh sent for Abram and got all up in his face and said, "What have you done to me?"

Pharaoh demanded, "Why didn't you tell me she was your wife? Why did you say, 'She is my sister,' and then you even went so far as to LET ME take her as MY wife? You better TAKE her and GET OUT of here. Get somewhere with yo old lyin' self!!"

Pharaoh ordered some of his men to make sure that Abram, Sarai and everything that Abram owned got out of Egypt, right away without any delay. Pharaoh was not playing games, he was wise, and he recognized when the plagues started and why. Pharaoh had to protect his people so he wanted Abram and everything pertaining to Abram out of his country, pronto, STAT!

Point to Ponder: Why was Abram so quick to forget the power of God and to lie and say that Sarai was his sister? Was he that short on faith? Was the altar that Abram set up between Bethel (holy place) and Ai (ruins and heaps) symbolic of the decision that he would need to make regarding being a man that stand s on the power of God and say to Pharaoh that Sarai was his wife or would he punk out and put Pharaoh in a place of ruin by saying Sarai was his sister? Good question!! Doesn't sound like Abram made the connection.

Take Away: When we are in situations that test us, as Abram was tested, let us find the strength of God and stand on His authority and do the right thing. Doing the right thing will add blessings to our life and choosing the wrong thing will not only harm us, but it will also harm others that we involve by making the wrong decision.

Prayer: Father we thank you for the strength to stand in the place of doing what is right.

Genesis 13: Abram and Lot Split Up

Abram left Egypt just as fast as he came! Abram, Sarai, and Lot, with all that they owned, traveled north into the Negev.

Abram was very rich in livestock, silver, and gold, even before Pharaoh gave him anything Abram already had more than enough. From the Negev, they continued, but they traveled in stages toward Bethel, and they finally pitched their tents between Bethel and Ai. They had actually camped there before they went to Egypt. This is the same place where Abram built the Altar to God and worshipped God. So Abram worshipped God again. This time Abram was probably giving God a thankful worship that Pharaoh did not kill him for lying about Sarai!

Lot, who was traveling with Abram, had also become very wealthy with flocks of sheep and goats, herds of cattle, and many tents. Many called Lot a "Clout Chaser", because they thought that he was riding on Abram's coat of fame, but this was not the case, Lot came along because Terah (his grandfather) brought him out of the Ur of Chaldeans, their hometown, with him.

Abram and Lot both had so many people and animals that they were too much for the land they settled on. They were using up all of the land's resources very quickly, because it was too much for that piece of land, which by the way was not little. You probably guessed it, neither Abram nor Lot wanted to leave that land because it had everything they needed. Of course we know when things get tight and space is limited, tempers flare. Abram and Lot's workers, who were taking care of the animals, began to argue and fight over the land.

Just to give you a broader picture, Abram and Lot were not the only ones living in that area; the Canaanites and Perizzites were also living in the land, so you know that things were truly tight.

Somebody had to be the bigger person. Enough is enough! FINALLY Abram said to Lot, "Hey man, come on now, we are better than this. Let's not allow THIS to come between us or our herdsmen. After all, we are day ones! Look around! This entire countryside is ours, take what you want. Choose any section of the land you want, and you can have it and I will go my way and you go your way. If you want the land to the left, then I'll take the land on the right. If you prefer the land on the right, then I'll go to the left."

Abram was being a peace maker and a negotiator. It wasn't about being right or wrong, but about finding the best working solution.

Lot said to himself, "Hmmmm what is the best of the land that I am looking at? What area has water and is fertile?"

Lot took a long look at the fertile plains of the Jordan (means descender or flowing down) Valley in the direction of Zoar (means little or insignificant). The whole area was well watered everywhere, like the garden of the LORD or the beautiful land of Egypt. Lot chose for himself the whole Jordan Valley to the east. He went there with his flocks and servants and parted company with his uncle Abram.

Since Canaan was what was left for Abram, that is where he settled.

Lot moved his tents to a place near Sodom (means burning) and settled among the cities of the plain. However, in all of Lot's thinking, looking and trying to get the best land for himself, he did not take into consideration what kind of people lived in the land near Sodom. What he chose was a place with people who were extremely wicked and that constantly sinned against the LORD.

After Lot left and Abram was alone, the LORD spoke to Abram and said, "Look as far as you can see in every direction—north and south, east and west. I am giving all of this land, as far as you can see, to you and your descendants as a permanent possession. And I will give you so many offspring that, like the dust of the earth, they cannot be counted! So, go on! Take a walk so that you can see what this land has to offer you. Walk the land in every direction, for I am giving it to you."

So Abram moved his camp to Hebron and settled near the oak grove belonging to Mamre (means strength and fatness). There Abram built another altar to the LORD.

Point to Ponder: When Lot was making his choice, did he made it off of surface appeal and what he thought was good according to what he could see? Did he even ask the Lord which land to take? Would he have made a better choice if he had his men to scout the area and see what it held, what kind of people etc., you know due diligence? Some times when we make decisions in haste, could they not be better decisions if we researched beforehand?

Take Away: Don't let simple disagreements tar apart important relationships with important people in your life, instead be a peace maker and negotiator like Abram. Abram saw that it was not about who was right or wrong, but about maintaining peace, love and harmony and he was blessed because of it.

Prayer: Lord today we ask that You would teach us how to be peace makers like Abram and we ask that You would give us wisdom in all of our decisions so that You may bless us, keep us and prosper us as our soul prospers.

Genesis 14: Abram's got Lot's back. Lot and King K.

About this time war broke out in the region. King Amraphel of Babylonia, King Arioch of Ellasar, King Kedorlaomer of Elam, and King Tidal of Goiim fought against King Bera of Sodom, King Birsha of Gomorrah, King Shinab of Admah, King Shemeber of Zeboiim, and the king of Bela (also called Zoar). It came down to four kings against five kings. What a battle and guess whose hasty decision landed them front and center, yes LOT!

The five kings joined forces in Siddim Valley (that is, the valley of the Dead Sea). For twelve years they had been subjected to King Kedorlaomer, but in the thirteenth year they had had enough and rebelled against him. Yes, this was the first insurrection like January 6, 2021. King Kedorlaomer was fierce and powerful. He, his men and ally armies would raid and plunder other tribes and cities for their valuables, especially those who were trying to be all up in his enemy's face.

One year later Kedorlaomer and his allies arrived and defeated the Rephaites (ancient race of giants) at Ashteroth-karnaim, the Zuzites at Ham, the Emites at Shaveh-kiriathaim, and the Horites at Mount Seir, all the way down to El Paran, which is at the edge of the wilderness. Then they made a 180 turn and went back to En-mishpat (now called Kadesh) and destroyed all who lived in the territory of the Amalekites, and also the Amorites living in Hazazon-tamar. They were some bad behind fighting warriors, killing and not taking hostages. King Kedorlaomer had a serious fighting spirit and a takeover spirit that wished to control everyone and everything.

Now the rebel kings of Sodom, Gomorrah, Admah, Zeboiim, and Bela (also called Zoar) prepared themselves for the war that was about to go down in the valley of the Dead Sea. They fought against King Kedorlaomer of Elam, King Tidal of Goiim, King Amraphel of Babylonia, and King Arioch of Ellasar. As I said four kings against five.

Now the Valley of the Dead Sea was a very strategic place because it was filled with tar pits. Tar pits are holes filled with very sticky tar. The tar is so thick that that the strongest person or animal could not escape. Tar pits are far, far worse than quicksand.

And as the army of the kings of Sodom and Gomorrah fled, some fell into the tar pits, while the rest escaped into the mountains. The victorious kings and their armies invaded and took everything from Sodom and Gomorrah as they headed home. They took everybody's things and food supplies. Yes, they took flat screens, microwaves, jewelry, any kind of electronic device, food and snacks. They were looking for car keys, but couldn't find them. As the story goes, they also captured Lot, yes, Abram's nephew who lived in Sodom. Not only did they capture him but they also stole everything that Lot owned.

As the saying goes, there is always a ram in the bush, one of Lot's men escaped, ran to Abram and told him everything that happened, especially how Lot was taken. As he was trying to catch his breath from running as fast as he could he said, "Sir Abram!! We knew that there was a big war going on and that the battle was hot, but we did not think we needed to evacuate and leave the city because we thought for sure that our armies would be able to protect Sodom and Gomorrah. But King K and his pose' pulled up and kicked our army's butt! And when the rest of our army saw what happened to the front line, you see what had happened was, the rest of the army ran off like little girls and left us. Little punks ran when things got heated. When they left us King K and his pose' pulled up on us and took Lot and everything he owned. I just barely got away."

Remember Abram was living near the oak grove belonging to Mamre the Amorite. Mamre and his relatives, Eshcol and Aner, were Abram's friends and they were well known for being fierce warriors.

When Abram heard what had happened to Lot, HIS nephew, he immediately pulled together 318 trained men! These men were not JUST trained men, but were men who knew the power of God because they were born and raised in Abram's house. Abram then went hard after King Kedorlaomer's army and he finally caught up with them at Dan.

Abram's plan was to divide his men and attack during the night. When Abram attacked at night, the strategy worked and King Kedorlaomer's army ran off like a pack of wounded dogs. Don't think that because they ran Abram was done with them, OH NO, Abram chased them as far as Hobah (means hiding place), which was 60 miles north of Damascus. Abram didn't care how far it was and where King K thought he could hide! King K had attacked and captured the wrong man that day and Abram wasn't having it! Abram caught up with King K, took back all of the goods that he had stolen, and the main thing is that Abram was able to get his nephew Lot AND all of his possessions, women and other captives. That was a glorious day and the people still talk about it now. They sing, "Abram beat King K this day, he chased him down, and took back everything that King K stole, oh no there wasn't a big enough hole, to hide King K that day!"

After Abram had shown King K who he was and more importantly who God was he went back and the king of Sodom ran down to the Valley of Shaveh, the King's valley, to thank him.

And Melchizedek, the king of Salem and a priest of the Almighty God, brought Abram some corn bread and red wine. Melchizedek knew how great of a task that Abram had just completed so he wanted to bless him with spoken word, so he said: "Abram you are blessed by our most high God who is the maker of earth and heaven. Yes, it was God Almighty who showed you how to win the war over King K. He showed you just how to do it and because you obeyed, you are victorious!! Blessed be God Most High, who has defeated your enemies for you."

Abram thought that there were no truer words spoken so he felt like he had to give Melchizedek something in return. So Abram gave Melchizedek ten percent of everything that he had brought back from the war. This is where the 10% tithe started that we always here in every church service. Ya know, "now it is time to bring your tithes and offering into the storehouse."

The king of Sodom, feeling some kind of way that Abram had been able to do what he and his army could not, said to Abram, "Give me back MY people who were captured. I don't care what you do with the rest, I just want my people back."

The King of Sodom needed someone to rule over and thought that he could use his authority to intimidate Abram and trying to act as if he were giving Abram something out of the kindness of his heart.

Abram looked at him and said, "I really don't need your people or any of these goods! I am blessed by God and have more than enough. I solemnly swear to the my LORD God Almighty, that I will not take so much as a crumb of bread, a single piece of clothing or a broken down designer shoe. You see I know people like you. You think that you are all that and IF I DID accept even a small piece of candy from you, you would tell everyone, what is truly in your heart, and that is that that you think you made me rich, when we all know that you don't have the funds to do so! Take your people and these riches! Boy bye!!"

Abram continued, "I will accept only what my young warriors have already eaten, and I request that you give a fair share of the goods to my friends who rode out with me to do what you and your army could not do. So give Aner, Eshcol, and Mamre a share of the goods."

Abram knew where his help came from and that was from the Lord his God! Abram was already rich and didn't need the goods or the headache that would come with them. Abram would not allow anyone to take God's glory. However, Abram did have a kind heart and wanted to bless his friends that stood by him and had his back in the battle with King K.

Point to Ponder: Why did Abram take 318 men? Is 318 significant or is it just the number that Abram needed to defeat King K, who had a large army and allies? Were these 318 men actually born to Abram or were they born to individuals that lived among or with Abram, after all God did tell Abram in the previous chapter. :... I will give you so many offspring that, like the dust of the earth, they cannot be counted."

Take Away: Just as Abram turned down the spoils of war so that the King of Sodom could not say that he made Abram rich when God had already done that, we should also be aware of the fact that everything is not for us and no one can take away from what God is doing in our lives and more especially take the Glory from God in the matter. Also, when friends, family and others assist us against the enemy or in any other matter let us not forget them when we receive our blessings.

Prayer: Lord we ask that you keep us humble and keep our hearts towards You, so that we may be wise enough to see exactly what the enemy is trying to do and to strategically defeat him and give You all the glory in the matter.

Genesis 15: Abram's Vision & God's 4Ever Contract

Sometime later, after all of the dust of the battle had settled, Abram had a vision and in this vision the LORD spoke to Abram and said, "Abram, man don't be scared! I will protect you, and give you a huge blessing."

In this vision Abram replied, "LORD, you know that I really do appreciate everything that you have done for me and what you are going to do, even though all of your blessings are good to me and for me, I do not have a son to leave all of your blessings to, I need a son."

And then Abram tried to use the tactics of manipulation and dry begging on the Lord. Abram said, "Since You have not given me any children, Eliezer of Damascus, one of my workers, will inherit all my wealth, all of the blessings that you have given me and that you are going to give me, ESPECIALLY, since You have given me no descendants, no sons of my own, no daughters of my own to leave all of this to. One of my servants will get it all. That just does not seem right."

Why did Abram think that one of his many blessings would not be an heir? Didn't Abram just sell the blessings of the Lord short with his narrow thinking?

Then the LORD said to Abram, "Come on now Abram! REALLY! NO, your servant will NOT be your heir, for you will have a son of your own to leave everything to."

Then the LORD took Abram outside and said to him, "Look up! Can you count all of the stars in the sky which I have placed there? Surely you cannot! Well, just think of this when I tell you that this is how many descendants you will have!"

You see how short Abram sold the Lord? Not just one heir, one son, but as many children as the stars in the sky! Do you think Abram owes the Lord a sincere and deeply heartfelt apology?

Abram was amazed at what the Lord said and showed him in this vision and Abram believed the LORD. NOW, because Abram believed so mightily in what the Lord said, the LORD counted him as righteous because of his faith.

Then the LORD reminded Abram what He had done for him just a little while ago, "I am the LORD who brought you out of Ur of the Chaldeans, your hometown, to give you this land as your possession."

Remember the Lord told Abram to leave the land of his fathers and he and Lot left, well this is what the Lord is speaking of?

But Abram being simple and short sighted, even after all the Lord had done for him, given him and showed him said to the Lord, "O Sovereign LORD, how can I be sure that I will actually possess it? This seems like a lot. How do I know that I will even live to receive it from you?"

The LORD said to Himself, "This man is something else, I have given him MY Word and yet he questions ME!"

So the Lord answered Abram and said, "Bring me a three-year-old female cow, a three-year-old female goat, a three-year-old ram, a turtledove, and a young pigeon."

So Abram went out and got all of the animals, brought them to the Lord and killed them. After he killed the animals, Abram cut each animal down the middle and laid the halves side by side; but for some reason he did not cut the birds in half. Because Abram had laid all of that fresh meat out in the open, some vultures came out of nowhere and thought that Abram had prepared a meal for them. The vultures tried their best to swoop down and snatch a meal, BUT Abram chased them away.

As the sun was going down and a cool breeze came across his face, Abram fell off to sleep, one of those snoring, slobbering sleeps and as he slept a terrifying darkness fell all around him and surrounded him like a blanket all over his body. And in this terrifying darkness the LORD gave Abram the not so pretty side of his blessing, the Lord said, "You can be sure that your offspring will be strangers in a foreign land, where they will be oppressed as slaves for 400 years. (Sounds like slavery that the Black people endured in America) But I will punish the nation that enslaves your offspring and in the end they will come away with great wealth. But as for you, you will die in peace and be buried at a ripe old age."

The Lord continued, "After four generations your descendants will return here, right here, to this land. I cannot destroy the Amorites right now to give your offspring this land, because right now the sins of the Amorites do not yet warrant their destruction. They are sinful but not so bad that I should destroy them right now. So be patient."

After the sun went down and it was dark once again, Abram saw a smoking firepot and a flaming torch pass between the halves of the bodies of the animals that he had killed for the Lord. This is the how the Lord established a covenant of promise that sealed the words and visions that he showed Abram.

The LORD made a covenant with Abram that day and said, "I have given this land to your offspring, all the way from the border of Egypt to the great Euphrates River. Yes, the land that is now occupied by the Kenites, Kenizzites, Kadmonites, Hittites, Perizzites, Rephaites, Amorites, Canaanites, Girgashites, and Jebusites."

That is ten tribes that would have to be destroyed for Abram's descendants to inhabit the land. Ten is often the number for tribulation. So before the descendants of Abram can inherit these lands, they will have to endure 400 years of slavery and hardship. WOW!!

Point to ponder: Why did the Lord want a three-year-old female cow, a three-year-old female goat, a three-year-old ram, a turtledove, and a young pigeon? What do they symbolize regarding sacrifice and offering unto the Lord? Abram cut each animal down the middle and laid the halves side by side; but he did not, cut the birds in half, why did he not cut the birds in half? Did the Lord command him to cut the other animals in half and leave the birds uncut? What might the vultures symbolize and why did they come out of nowhere and what allowed Abram to chase them away? This verse is highly symbolic.

Take away: No matter what God promises you, as long as you are in Him and He is in you, those promises are Yes and Amen in Him. Do not be like Abram and doubt God so much that a covenant or contract is needed to appease your lack of faith. Remember what God has already done for you to encourage your faith and what He is going to do. When you have blessings from the Lord, watch over them so that he enemy (vultures) does not try to swoop in and take them away. Be careful and watch for danger signs ahead.

Prayer: Lord we ask today that we have the faith to believe in the substance of those things that are hoped for and to believe in the evidence of the unseen. Let us always maintain a heart of faith towards You as Your heart is for us. We ask for the ability to spot the tricks of the enemy before they are launched and to destroy any tactics or strategies of the enemy.

Genesis 16: The Wife and the Side Chick

The Lord had made a promise to Abram that he would have a son, an heir, someone to leave all of his wealth to. Well, let us go and see how this plays out.

Abram's wife was named Sarai, and she had not been able to get pregnant and have children. Sarai knew that Abram wanted a son and God knows that the two tried on a regular basis to get Sarai pregnant.

Back in those days men wanted a son to leave their wealth to. Sarai probably heard Abram murmuring in his sleep about not having a son. So Sarai not knowing the vision that Abram had, thought that she would take matters into her own hands. Oh, my, what a dangerous thing to do!

Sarai had an Egyptian servant named Hagar and thought that Hagar should be a surrogate mother, so Sarai said to Abram, "No matter how hard we try to have a baby, it does not seem to be the Lord's will at this time. It's just not happening like we want it to. So what if I give you Hagar to sleep with, and hopefully you can have a son with her in my place. I am actually giving you permission to sleep with her. Perhaps I can have children through her."

Doesn't this level of manipulation sound like Adam and Eve and the tree in the garden? Was Sarai trying to see if the problem of not being able to get pregnant was actually her physical problem or by giving Hagar to Abram to sleep with was she trying to see if Abram had bad sperm and the problem was not hers alone? Why does Sarai think that the Lord has prevented her from having children? I guess since there were no fertility specialist in that era of time, we will never know. Back to the story!

Now of course, being a man, Abram agreed with Sarai's proposal. Abram thought, "I get my cake and Ice cream with my bae's permission!"

My question is, "WHY" did Abram so quickly forget the vision and promises of the Lord and agree to take Hagar to sleep with and to have a son with? Hmmm. I believe that we all know why!

Sarai, Abram's wife, took Hagar the Egyptian servant and gave her to Abram as a wife. Not just to sleep with, but as a wife. All of this happened ten years after Abram decided to live in the land of Canaan. You see back in those days when a man and woman had sexual intercourse, that made them husband and wife. If that were the rule today it would be a hot mess!

Abram was a spiritual man, but he was yet still a man and Abram had sexual relations with Hagar, and of course, as expected, she became pregnant.

One thing that Sarai did not count on is that Hagar would no longer consider herself as a servant, especially since she just became Abram's wife with Sarai's permission and more especially now that she is pregnant with Abram's child. SOOOO when Hagar knew she was pregnant, she began to treat Sarai like she was better than Sarai and like Sarai was worthless because she couldn't get pregnant for Abram. Hagar thought in her mind that she was better than Sarai because she became pregnant for Abram right away and 10 years into their marriage, Sarai still had not become pregnant.

Hagar thought to herself, "I slept with Abram ONE time and I, the low servant, can give him what he wants! Sarai! Gurl, you need to go sit down somewhere with your broken poo-nani."

Then Sarai started acting like Eve and said to Abram, "This is all your fault! I gave you Hagar to sleep with and to get you that son that you can't stop talking about, and look at her now! Just look at her! She is beside herself because she is pregnant and she treats ME, of all people, like I am nothing. You betta get yo girl, cause I am not going to put up with this mess, pregnant or not! I am about five seconds offa her."

Then Sarai took it a step further and said, "The LORD will show you who's wrong in this picture!! He will show you if it is YOU or me and I guarantee you that it is not ME!"

Now you know that with Sarai's statement she really felt that Abram was wrong and should have turned Hagar away and not had sex with her.

Abram thought about it and said, "Look, SARAI, she is YOUR servant! YOU gave HER to ME, so YOU deal with HER as YOU see fit."

And with those words Sarai and Hagar were at war and of course Sarai won because as Abram's first wife and everyone else in the camp knowing that Sarai was in charge, poor Hagar didn't stand a chance. It was so bad that Hagar actually packed up and left the camp.

Sarai and Abram were not concerned that Hagar was gone. Sarai was glad that the contemptuous heifer was gone and Abram was glad because he didn't have to hear the arguing and Sarai's nagging at him about Hagar. BUT the Lord was concerned and sent an angel to find Hagar. The angel found Hagar beside a spring of water in the wilderness, along the road to Shur.

The angel said to Hagar, "Hagar, Sarai's servant, what are you doing out here all alone? Where have you come from, and where are you planning on going?"

Notice how the angel calls her servant. That was to let her know that she was not greater than Sarai, because the Lord gave Sarai to Abram. The Lord did not give Hagar to Abram, Sarai did and Sarai did not have the authority to do so.

Hagar said, "I'm getting away from that crazy heifer named Sarai. I just can't! To stay there and deal with her craziness is far too much for me. Sarai told me to sleep with Abram, HER husband. She gave me to Abram as his WIFE and now that I am pregnant with his child she gets jealous and starts treating me like I am less than HIS pregnant wife, when it was all her idea to start with! I am the pregnant one, she should step back."

The angel of the LORD said to her, "You betta get yourself up from here and go back to Sarai and Abram and act like you have some sense. Submit yourself to her authority. Do not go back there acting like you all that and have authority over her because you are pregnant. You do not have authority over her!"

Then he added, "I will give you more children than you can count. You are now pregnant and you WILL give birth to a son. When you have the boy, name him Ishmael (which means 'God hears'), for the LORD has heard your cry of distress. Ishmael, this son of yours, will be a wild man, very untamed! He will raise his fist against everyone, and everyone will be against him. Yes, he will live with a bitter attitude against all his relatives."

After hearing this and receiving these specific instructions and insight, Hagar used another name to refer to the LORD, who had spoken to her. She said, "**You, God, have seen me.**"

And she added, "Have I truly seen my God who sees me?"

Now because of this experience, the well or spring where the angel of the Lord found Hagar was named Beer-lahai-roi (which means "well of the Living One who sees me"). It can still be found between Kadesh and Bered.

So, Hagar went back, humbled herself before Abram and Sarai and later had the baby boy. She made sure that Abram named the boy Ishmael. Abram was **eighty-six years** old when Ishmael was born. Eighty-six was the new 36!!

Point to Ponder: Why didn't Abram tell Sarai about the vision and conversation he had with the Lord regarding a son? By Abram agreeing to sleep with Hagar to have a son, did that show his lack of faith or did he think that this was how the Lord was going to give him a son? Did Sarai step out of bounds by giving Hagar to Abram or was she in God's plan for Abram to have a son?

Take away: Communication with God is mandatory in order to know what He has for your life and if you are married share these visions and communications with your spouse especially when it concerns both of you. When the Lord shows you His promises for your life, ask Him for direction and guidance, do not take things into your own hands and suffer the consequences.

Prayer: Lord we thank You for writing the pages of our lives before we were born and we ask that You would direct us to the path that leads us to our destiny in You. Give Your angels charge over us so that we do not hurt ourselves as we walk out this path.

Genesis 17: Abram or is it Abraham?

After all of the drama with Sarai and Hagar and when Abram turned 99 years of age, once again the LORD wanted to have conversation with Abram. God said, "I am El-Shaddai, 'God Almighty.' Serve me faithfully and live a blameless life and I will make an agreement with you, by which I will guarantee to give you a countless family tree."

When Abram heard this he fell face down on the ground and God said to him, "This is my agreement with you: I will make you the father of a multitude of nations! AND I am changing your name. Your name will no longer be Abram, but your name will now be Abraham, for you will be the father of many nations. I will make you extremely fruitful. Your descendants will become many nations, and kings will be among them!"

The Lord continued, "I will confirm my agreement with you and your offspring that come after you, from generation to generation. This is the everlasting agreement: I will always be your God and the God of your descendants after you. And I will give the entire land of Canaan, where you now live as a foreigner, to you and your descendants. It will be their possession forever, and I will always be their God."

God continued, "Your responsibility is to obey the terms of the agreement. You and all your offspring will always have this continual responsibility. This is the agreement that you and your descendants must keep: each male among and you must be circumcised (remove the top skin from their penis). You must cut off the flesh of your top skin as a sign of your obedience to this agreement. From generation to generation, every male child must be circumcised on the eighth day after his birth. This applies not only to members of your family but also to the servants born in your household and the immigrant servants whom you have purchased. All must be circumcised. Your bodies will bear this mark. Any male who fails to be circumcised will be cut off from everyone else for breaking this agreement."

Then God said to Abraham, "Regarding Sarai, your wife—her name will no longer be Sarai, but from now on her name will be Sarah. And even though she took matters into her own hands, I will keep my promise to you and give you a son from her! Yes, I will bless her richly, and she will become the mother of many! Kings of nations and nations will be among her descendants."

Now after hearing the Lord say this, Abraham bowed down to the ground. However this WAS unbelievable to Abraham, after all he was 100 years old and Sarah was 90 years old. Abraham laughed quietly to himself. Abraham could no longer contain it and thought to himself, "How can I become a father at the age of 100, come on now?"

And he continued in thought to himself by saying, "And certainly Sarah has not had any children all of these years, and we sho been trying, so how in the world can Sarah get pregnant and a have a baby when she is ninety years old, this is unreal?"

So Abraham could no longer control himself and said to God, "Ishmael, the boy I had by Hagar my side chick, is he included in this blessing?"

This was a strange question since Ishmael's mother is Hagar and was already born outside of the covenant/agreement that God had just made with Abraham, BUT this was Abraham's respectful way of saying that he did not believe the Lord.

God replied, "No, now. Sarah, your wife, WILL give you a baby boy. You will name him Isaac, and I will confirm my covenant with him and his descendants as an everlasting covenant. As for Ishmael, I will bless him also, just as you have asked. I will make him extremely fruitful and multiply his descendants. Twelve of his children will become kings and Ishmael will become a great nation through him. HOWEVER, my agreement with YOU will only be confirmed with Isaac, who will be born to you and Sarah about this time next year."

When God had finished speaking, he left so that Abraham could think about everything that He had said.

The very day of this conversation became a very painful day for the men in Abraham's camp because on that same day Abraham took his son, Ishmael, and every male in his household, including those born there and those he had purchased and ABRAHAM circumcised them. Abraham performed the circumcision himself, this way he knew that he had fulfilled his portion of the agreement with God. Abraham cut off their top skin, just as God had told him, and was very careful with the sharp knife so that he did not cut or remove anything else! Abraham was ninety-nine years old when he was circumcised.

Today circumcision normally happens to nearly every male child at birth. I have heard nurses refer to the procedure as 'getting the wiener clipped.'

Abraham was 99 and Ishmael, his son, was thirteen. Both Abraham and his son, Ishmael, were circumcised on that same day, along with all the other men and boys under Abrahams' roof, whether they were born there or were purchased. ERBODY was circumcised that day. It's a good thing that a war didn't break out, because Abraham and his camp would have surely lost the fight in the condition they were in!

Point to Ponder: Why did God change Abraham and Sarah's name? Was this a spiritual upgrade? Why did Abraham find it so hard to believe that He and Sarah would have a baby at this same time next year, but found it easy to go back and circumcise all of the males? Why were women not included in this covenant or were they included by Sarah having a son from Abraham's circumcised seed? Why was circumcision in the United States of America not a common practice until after World War 1?

Take away: As we are all included in this covenant it is our responsibility to be obedient the terms of the covenant and to pass this obedience down that we may become fruitful in all areas of our lives.

Prayer: Father we thank you today that You saw fit to make an everlasting covenant and to include us, and we thank You that you had us in mind, even at the time of making the covenant with Abraham. We ask that You would give us the power and strength to find the place our place this agreement. We further ask that You empower us to be continual covenant keepers as You have been and continue to be a covenant keeping God.

Genesis 18: Sarah laughs at and Lies to God

The Lord and Abraham had a close relationship and often fellowshipped. Once again the LORD wanted to have conversation with Abraham and this time it was in the middle of the day when it was the hottest outside. It was so hot outside that Abraham did not go any further than the doorway of his tent. Abraham looked around to survey his camp and when he looked further out he noticed three men standing there. They did not look suspect or like they came to do harm so Abraham ran over to say hello and see what was going on. When he approached them he bent his head low to the ground and said, "Welcome. Now that I am closer to you I am able to recognize who you are!"

That was a powerful statement. Just a quick question before moving on, does that mean the closer we are to God the more we will recognize Him? Hmmmm?

Now we know that this was a different time and era, because today if three men were seen standing close to someone else's property the first reaction would be to defend yourself not to run and greet them, and to have your phone in hand ready to record or call 911, depending on their actions. Now if they seemed hostile, it would call for other measures, but that is today's world where strangers are usually scheming and plotting!!

Abraham truly recognized that these were no ordinary three men, but the Father, Son and Holy Spirit in the flesh with two angels! Abraham humbled himself and said, "My Lord, I see You and if it is ok with You, would You please stop here for just a little while? It's hot as hades out here, so please sit here and rest under the shade of this tree and I will get one of my servants to bring some water for You to wash the dust off Your feet and some lotion to soothe them and keep them from being ashy. This will also help to cool You down. More especially since you have graced me with your presence I feel honored, so please let me prepare some good ole comfort soul food to fill Your empty stomach's and strengthen You before You go Your way."

The three men looked at each other and thought, this is awfully kind of him and said "All right now!! How did you know? Man you have checked all the items on the list to make this the place to be. That sounds great!"

Abraham said to Sarah, "Hey baby! Hurry! Get three large measures of your best flour, knead it into dough, and bake some bread, better yet make some honey butter cornbread."

Then Abraham ran out to where he kept his animals and chose a tender baby calf and gave it to his servant and said, "Put the Chef's touch on this but cook it quickly. Make sure that it is well seasoned and cooked in coconut milk so that it will be tasty and tender."

When the food was ready, Abraham took the honey butter corn bread, some vegetables and the tender beef and he served it to the men. Abraham was so honored by their presence that he did not eat with them, but he decided to wait for them to finish eating under the shade of one of the other big trees.

While all of this was going on the three men were taking note of everything that Abraham had and eventually asked Abraham, "Where is your wife Sarah? She was here just a few seconds ago."

Abraham thought that this was a bit suspect because he never did mention Sarah's name, he only called her baby in front of them, but then he remembered who they were and answered them by saying, "She's went back inside of the tent."

One of the men replied, "I will return to you about this time next year, and your wife, Sarah, will have a son!"

From this exchange and how Abraham reacted when he first saw the men, it is apparent that Abraham recognized these three men for who they were. Not just men, but God and His messengers.

Sarah was in the tent, and of course she was ear hustling on the conversation as usual! She was curious as to who they were, especially since they didn't get much company or people stopping by way out there in the country. She was trying hard to hear what was going on and what was being said. She thought to herself, "I certainly hope that these three men are not up to something bad cause me and Abraham are too old to be fighting."

Abraham and Sarah were both very old by this time, and Sarah was too old to even think about having a child. So when Sarah did finally hear the conversation clearly and heard one of the men say that she would have a son this time next year, she laughed hard, but silently to herself and said, "How in the world can an old worn-out woman like me enjoy sex with my husband AND have a baby too?"

Sarah laughed some more and then said, "How can I enjoy such intimate pleasure with Abraham?! Just look at Abraham, he is even older than me?"

We have learned from other stories that the LORD knows and hears everything so He said to Abraham, "Why is Sarah in the tent laughing? I also heard her say, 'How in the world can an old worn-out woman like me enjoy sex with my husband AND have a baby too?'

The Lord continued and said, "Do you think that giving you and Sarah a baby is too hard for ME? You hold that thought, but best believe that when I return about this same time next year, you and Sarah WILL have a son. Best believe!"

Sarah and Abraham were astonished to hear the Lord repeat what Sarah said and to know that she laughed and thought that the message from the man was absurd and crazy.

Sarah suddenly became afraid, and had the nerve to lie to God, and denied laughing and said, "Who me? I didn't laugh. You must have heard one of the servants carrying on."

But the LORD said, "No, it clearly was you!! You were the one that I heard laughing."

After all of this, and when the men finished enjoying their meal and time of rest under the shade tree, they got up and started to walk toward Sodom. As they left, Abraham went with them to wish them a farewell.

The Lord thought and asked himself, "Should I keep my plan from Abraham? Should I tell him what's about to go down in Sodom and Gomorrah? I know that

Abraham will most certainly become a great and mighty nation, and all the nations of the earth will be blessed through him, but I still don't know if I should tell him. I have singled him out so that he will direct his sons and their families to keep the way of the LORD by doing what is right according to our agreement and I will do for Abraham all that I have promised."

With that in mind, the LORD decided to tell Abraham the following, "Abraham, look, the reason that I am here is because the cries of all that sin from the cities of Sodom and Gomorrah have reached my ears. It is so much sin that I constantly hear it boldly crying out as if to say that I won't do anything about it! So, I am going down there to see if their actions are as wicked as I have heard. I need to check this out for myself, up close and in person because I don't wanna just wipe them out without TRULY knowing what is going on."

Upon hearing the Lord tell Abraham his plan, the other two men turned and headed toward Sodom, but Abraham and the Lord continued their conversation. Abraham, thought about what the Lord said and thought about his nephew Lot being in Sodom and Gomorrah. Abraham thought I must try and change the Lord's mind, so Abraham went to the Lord and said, "Lord, um, I understand your plan and why you have this plan but, hypothetically speaking, will you destroy the good with the wicked? What if in fact you find fifty good people living in the city—will you still destroy everyone, even the fifty?"

Abraham continued, "Lord, I think that we have become pretty close and would you really do such a thing, destroy the good along with the wicked? REALLY? I don't understand why you would treat the good people and the wicked people exactly the same! Surely you wouldn't do that! Now, I know that You are the Judge of all the earth, but shouldn't you take this into consideration?"

The Lord heard Abraham and decided to go along with Abraham's attempt to negotiate and persuade Him to abort his plan. The LORD replied with an eye roll, "If I find fifty good people in the city, I will not destroy the city just because they are there."

Hmmm. Abraham thought, since I got the Lord to say that he wouldn't destroy it for 50 good people, let me see just how far I can go with this. Then Abraham spoke again, "Since we are talking, can we talk a little more? I realize that I am but dust and ashes, but suppose, just suppose there are only forty-five good people rather than fifty? Will you still destroy the whole city because it is five short of fifty good people?"

The Lord laughed to Himself and said, "Okay, I will not destroy it if I find forty-five good people there."

Abraham started feeling real good about himself and pressed the issue further and said, "What if there are only forty good people?"

And the LORD replied, "Alright then, I will not destroy it for forty good people."

Abraham did not know what to do with himself at this point, he felt like he was on a roll and was negotiating with the Lord. He thought to himself, "No one will ever believe that I am negotiating with God Himself!"

Abraham said to the Lord, "Uh Lord. Please don't get upset with me and I realize that I am probably getting on your nerves right about now, BUT what if there are only thirty good people there in the city?"

And the LORD replied, "You're Okay, You're not getting on my nerves. If there are only thirty good people I will not destroy the city."

Now the Lord knew that Abraham was not quite finished yet with this line of questioning and attempt to negotiate. So the Lord went along with it. Then Abraham said to himself let me try this again, the Lord is going along with me so he spoke out and said, "Since we are talking and I since I am pressing the issue, to You, my Lord this far, may I please continue?

Abraham did not give the Lord a chance to answer him he just asked the next question, "Suppose it's only twenty good God fearing people there?"

And the LORD replied, "Then I will not destroy it for the twenty good God fearing people that are there."

The Lord was seeing just how far Abraham would take it.

Finally, Abraham said to himself, let me give it one final try, "Lord, please, please don't be angry or agitated with me, BUUUTTTT what if, just what if it's only, say ten righteous, good, praying, God fearing people, instead of the original fifty? Forty less? What will happen then?"

And the LORD replied, "Then I will not destroy it for the sake of the ten righteous, good, praying, and God fearing people."

The LORD had had enough of this conversation with Abraham so He went on his way to take do what He had to do, and Abraham went back to his tent. On Abraham's way back he was feeling good and felt like he was "da man" because he was able to talk with and negotiate with God. Abraham took one step and stopped and said, "WOW!! Did that just happen? I can't wait to get home and tell Sarah about this! WOW, just WOW."

And Abraham went on his way smiling and laughing all the way home.

Point to Ponder: How did Abraham recognize that the three men were not strangers, but were sent of God or was he just nice and hospitable to everyone? Why didn't Sarah recognize the Word about her having a child next year as a confirmation to what the Lord told Abraham earlier? Had Abraham not told her, as of yet, what the Lord said to him?

Take Away: The Lord was very patient with Abraham as he attempted to negotiate with Him. Do you think that if Abraham had kept going that he would have been able to save Sodom from being destroyed for the sake of Lot and his family?

Prayer: Father we thank you for giving us wisdom to recognize You and those that You send to us and that we would show them kindness and hospitality. We ask for the ability to speak with You in all humility and to know when Your goal in the conversation has been reached. Let us not fall short.

Genesis 19: A Nosey Wife & 2 "JUST NASTY" Daughters

That evening when the two angels (known in the previous chapter as the two men) arrived at the entrance to the city of Sodom, Lot, Abraham's nephew, was sitting there, and when he looked up and saw them, he immediately rose to his feet, bowed his head and welcomed them. Lot was so happy to see someone other than the wicked people of Sodom that he cheerfully welcomed them and bowed his head to the ground in gratitude. Lot greeted the men the same way that Abraham had greeted them.

Lot said, "Welcome, welcome, welcome, my God sent lords! Let me invite you to come to my house and wash the dirt and dust off your feet from your travels. I invite you to be MY guests for the night and then you can get up early in the morning, well rested and fed and continue your journey."

The two angels answered Lot and said, "Naw, that's alright. We will just stay right here and sleep out here in the city square."

The men wanted to observe what goes on in the city, to hear and see the cries of sin, they did not come to make friends or hang out; these men were on a mission!!

Lot thought to himself, "These two men have no idea of what this city is like, I must convince them to come with me because wickedness comes out at night. If they stay here especially at night, they are in for a bad thuggish surprise and I already know that something is gonna happen to them. I can't let them to stay out here tonight or any other night, they gotta come with me."

So Lot insisted once again and said, "Believe me when I tell you that you DO NOT want to stay out here in THIS Square tonight, or any other night. The Wicked Come out at night and it ain't no tellin' what they will try to do to you."

So after hearing Lot, the two men looked at each other and decided that maybe they should listen, after all he is from here and knows better than we do what the goings on are around here. So they went with Lot.

Lot prepared a feast, a smorgasbord buffet for the two men. He had fresh homemade honey butter cornbread without yeast, greens, lima beans, stewed tomatoes, yellow rice, and some Cornish hens and of course some sweet potato candied yams. They all sat down and enjoyed the meal.

However, before they settled down for the night and just as Lot said, night fell and the wicked came out in full force. All the men of Sodom, young and old, came from all over the city, from 5th Avenue and MLK Drive, Blue Street and Myrtle Avenue and Jefferson Avenue and Frost Street and surrounded the house. They started yelling and shouting to Lot saying, "Where them men that we saw in the city square earlier? We saw you talking to them and we saw them come to your house!! Bruh, BRUH, you better open your door and let them come out. Oh yeah, send them out cause we ARE going to gang rape them THIS night and do whatever else we want to them!"

These men were on assignment from Satan himself. Satan knew that the two men came to shut down his sinful, wicked and evil reign over the city of Sodom and

Gomorrah, so he wanted to try and contaminate their spirit and destroy their physical bodies.

After Lot heard what wicked words the men were speaking to him he went outside to try and talk some sense into these demons. We all know that you can't talk sensibly to demons, the only thing they understand is the name of Jesus, fasting and praying, BUT Lot tried anyways. He stepped out and slammed the door behind him to get the crazy men's attention and he began to plead with them saying, "Hey, hey, hey! My bru-thers! Why! Why would you want to gang rape these men, that's evil, vile and disgusting? Please get off of my property, keep it moving and leave me and my guests alone. I am begging you to not do this!"

Lot thought that since they weren't leaving he needed to offer them an alternative to raping the two men, so he said, "Now I know that you have seen my two pretty daughters around town, well they are VIRGINS! What if I bring them out to you, instead of the two men, and let you have your way with them? You can do whatever you would like to do to them instead of these two men. How does that sound? I ask that you forget about the two men, because they are my guests and under my care and protection. On the other side of this I just know that you don't want me to call my uncle Abraham?! You do remember what happen to King K, when he attacked me and took my possessions. I thought so, he chased him down and did what he does!! Think about that for a moment."

Lot's daughters overheard what Lot, their father said to the men about them. The oldest daughter said to her younger sister, "Did you hear what father just said! He told all of those men that we are virgins and that he would give us to them to do what they wanted to do with us! He said because the two men were under his care and protection, WELL AREN'T WE, HIS DAUGHTERS, UNDER HIS CARE AND PROTECTION!! I guess we know how he feels about us."

There was one man in the group of men in front of Lot's house that just wanted to act a pure fool because he wanted what he wanted and for no other reason than to feel like he has power. There is usually always on in the bunch somewhere ready to act like Satan's child! Anyways, this person said, "Y'all Stand back! This man, THIS MAN named Lot, came to OUR town as an outsider, and now he has the nerve, the gall and audacity to try and act like he knows us! Who made him judge and king? He really thinks that he can tell us what to do! I don't think so."

Then he turned to address Lot and said, "If you do not move yo narrow behind out of the way, we can do the same thing to you that we are going to do to the two men! Maybe we will do far worse to you than what we are going to do to those two men!"

And then the crowd of men lunged towards Lot and tried to rush the door as if they were rushing the stage at a concert or something. They tried hard to break down the door to Lot's house. These men just didn't know the power that they were dealing with and going up against, but they fo sho found out.

The two men/angels inside were very much aware of what was going on outside and they knew this in advance of coming to Sodom that this would take place, so the two angels opened the door, grabbed Lot and yanked him back inside of the house, closed and bolted the door. But that wasn't all that the two angels did, they also blinded every man that was on the other side of the door! All of the men, young and old, who were outside of the house trying to get in were blinded and because they could not see the men stopped trying to get in. They couldn't even find the door, the door handle or the house, they were blind!! They didn't have a choice but to retreat and grope in the dark trying to find their way home.

I can hear them now blaming each other and especially blaming the loud mouthed man saying, "Dude, look what you did and what you got us into. We knew that we shouldn't have listened to you and your foolishness. You're the original idiot! Now I can't even see how to get home. You just wait until I get my sight back, if I do, I am coming for you and yours."

While the men were outside stumbling about the angels questioned Lot asking, "Do you have any other relatives living in this city right now at this time? If you do you MUST get them out of this place; your sons-in-law, sons, daughters, or anyone else related to you."

Lot asked, "Why, what's going on?"

The two angels said, "We are about to completely destroy this city. The cries of bold and wicked sin against this place is so great that the sounds have reached the LORD, and He has sent us here to destroy this place. That is why those men came here thinking they were going to destroy us, they didn't realize that they were being used by the devil, because the devil knew what our assignment was and he didn't want his den of sin shut down and his reign here to end."

After Lot heard this it was like a fire was lit under him! He rushed out to tell his daughters' fiancés, "Quick, get out of the city! The LORD is about to destroy it."

But of course like in Noah's day, the young men thought he was only joking, didn't believe him and went on about their business saying, "Lot has jokes today! Oh yes he does. He is just too funny at times! The Lord is about to destroy the city, now that's a good one!!"

Early the next morning, right at about the break of dawn, well at daybreak, the two angels pressed Lot even more saying, "Why are you still here?! You had better hurry up and get your wife and your two daughters and GET OUT!! It is about to go down and if you do not leave right now you will be caught up and destroyed as we destroy this wicked city!"

Of course Lot was concerned about everyone else and how he could get them out and wasn't moving fast enough, so the angels grabbed his hand and the hands of his wife and two daughters and took them outside of the city into safety.

The Lord was merciful and the Lord remembered the conversation that Abraham had asking if He finds 10 righteous souls will he save the city. When they were safely out of the city, one of the angels ordered them by saying, "Run for your lives! And don't look back at what is going on and most certainly do not stop anywhere in this valley! Just keep it moving and run to the mountains, or you WILL be taken out and destroyed also!"

Lot began to beg again because he knew that he was too scared to go into the mountains alone, with just his family so he said, "On no! 1 I just can't go to the mountains. NO, not the mountains, any place but there. You have been so gracious and kind to me and my family and saved our lives, but I cannot go to the mountains. There are only bad things waiting for me if I go there and I know that I would die there sooner than later. However, there is a small village that is closer than the mountains and I would feel safer there because it is small, so may we please go there instead; don't you see how small it is? If we go there I probably won't be killed and die earlier than I should."

The angel said, "Alright, alright! I will grant your request. I will allow you to go there and I will not destroy the little small village. BUT YOU GOTTA STOP WASTING TIME! YOU MUST HURRY! Go to the small village with a quickness because I cannot begin the destruction until you arrive there."

The name of the village was Zoar, which means, "Little place."

Lot reached the village just as the sun was rising over the horizon and once Lot and his family were there fire and burning sulfur fell from the sky onto Sodom just like rain. And according to the local five o'clock morning news the same thing was happening in Gomorrah.

The Lord utterly destroyed both Sodom and Gomorrah, along with the other cities and villages that were participating in the sinful activities. He wiped out all the people, the buildings and even the food that was growing. The Lord wiped every bit of evil and wickedness in those cities that day.

Lot's wife was a very nosey woman and had a short memory because she forgot that the angels told them not to look back, so between being nosey trying to see what was going down and her short memory, as she followed behind Lot she looked back and the moment she look back she turned into a pillar of salt! She was frozen in place like a statue and became a salt lick for horses!

Hey, she was warned but she let her nosiness bring a bitter end to her life. Even still, that was very hard for Lot and his daughters to see this and to lose her after the angels had been so kind to rush them all out to safety. That was a great loss especially, since the other people they knew would not heed Lot's warning to leave the city and were destroyed. All that they had was each other.

Abraham knew that it was about that time for the Lord to destroy Sodom, so he got up early that morning and hurried out to the place where he had been negotiating with the Lord. He looked over toward Sodom and Gomorrah and could see big thick black columns of smoke rising from the cities like smoke from a forest fire. Abraham could look at the destruction because he was not from Sodom and the angels did not tell him not to look back.

But in all of the destruction and death, God had listened to and remembered Abraham's request and kept Lot and his family safe, by having the angels move Lot and his family to safety.

After all of the destruction, Lot left Zoar, the small village, because he was afraid of the people there. It seems that lot makes bad choices when it comes to places to live. He never went to see what the small village was like, just like he did when he moved his family to Sodom. He and his daughters went to live in a cave in the mountains. Isn't that something, hmm? Lot went to live in the very place the angels told him to go to in the first place!

There was nothing really to do in the mountains and living in a cave was certainly no fun. There was no one there but Lot and his two daughters. There was no internet, cable or jail broken Fire stick so the girls were antsy and had idle minds. Their minds were so idle that evil thoughts entered, started to control them and they just went with the flow. It wasn't too long after they got settled in the cave that the oldest sister said to the youngest, "You know what? We are virgins and there are no men anywhere in this entire area, so we can't get married and start a family like everyone else. And our father will soon be too old to have children. Do you remember that he was willing to give us to that crazy demon mob?! He even told them that we were virgins and they could have their way with us, do whatever they wanted to do to us. I didn't understand how he could offer us up like that! So let's get him drunk with wine, and then we will have sex and have our way with him. That way he can suffer what he was going to let those men do to us and most importantly we will be able to have children and keep the family going through having sex with daddy."

OMG! Yuck!! Do you think that the ways of Sodom and Gomorrah had rubbed off on Lot's two daughters and that Satan was exacting revenge on Lot for not letting those two men come out so that they could be gang raped and destroyed by the crowd?

So later on that night after they had given Lot a wonderful dinner and too much wine the two wicked daughters carried out their plan and made sure that their father, Lot, was out of his mind drunk with wine. That wasn't hard to do, because Lot was in his feelings about losing his wife and about having to go to the mountains to live.

The older evil minded daughter went in and had sex with her father. She did all manner of things to him to exact revenge. Lot was too drunk to be aware of having sex with his daughter. He didn't know that she got into his bed or when she left. He HAD to be awfully drunk not to know that he was sleeping with his daughter!!

The next morning the older daughter said to her younger sister, "Gurl, I had sex with daddy last night. I got him really drunk and did all kinds of things to him. I am sure that I will get pregnant after that. I propose that we get him drunk, really drunk again tonight, so that you can go in and do the same thing that I did last night. I will coach you on what to do, okay? That way we can both get pregnant by daddy and start our own family!"

So once again and for a second night, the two wicked daughters got their father, Lot, drunk with red, red wine! This time the younger daughter went in and had sex with him and did to him what the older daughter showed her to do. Just as with the oldest daughter, Lot was so drunk that he did not know that the he slept with his younger daughter, he did not know when she came to his bed or when she left.

How drunk was he?! What in the world did they give Lot? Sounds like some seriously strong wine for him not to know that he was having sex with his own daughters. Yes this is INCEST!!

As a result, and as planned, both of Lot's daughters became pregnant. That's just too nasty! They were pregnant by their own father! When the older daughter gave birth to her son, she named him Moab, which means the seed of the father. Moab became the ancestor of the Moabite nation. The just too nasty daughters had their sons about the same time. So when the younger daughter gave birth to her son, she named him Ben-ammi. He became the ancestor of the nation now known as the Ammonites.

This chapter is something "tuther" as my father would say. Modern day soap operas and night time television series have nothing on this chapter!!

Point (s) to Ponder: Why did Lot and his family have to go to the mountains instead of with Abraham? Why did Lot go to Zoar instead of the mountains that he eventually went to? Did the destruction that Lot feared in the mountains have anything to do with his daughters and what they did to him? Why was Lot so drunk that he did not know he was having sex with his daughters? Did he question himself once he realized that his daughters were pregnant and there were no other men around but him? Were the men in Sodom homosexuals or were they just evil men being used by Satan to commit the evil act of gang rape; against the angels, to try and dirty the spirit of the two men and destroy their physical bodies? Is there far more to this than meets the eye? Why is this particular story so often quoted and used against homosexuals when in fact it has nothing to do with homosexuality at all but more to do with incest? Isn't Judges 19 and the city of Gibeah the exact same story, why is it never mentioned?

Take away: When we receive instructions not to look back at a situation, place or person does it hinder us and stifle our growth when we do look back, just as it did Lot's wife? We can't move forward into the blessings of the Lord by looking back.

Prayer: Father we thank You today and ask that You would count us worthy and save us from destruction as You did Lot and his family. Give us the ability to live righteous and blameless lives that are pleasing to You.

Genesis 20: Two Time Liars.

After the Lord destroyed Sodom and Gomorrah and Lot had moved into the mountains, Abraham decided to move also to area of Negev in the neighborhood of Kadesh and Shur. However he did live in Gerar for a bit. Here again Abraham was fearful and unsure of the people in Gerar so he lied A-GAIN and told everyone that Sarah, his wifey, was his sister. He blatantly lied and misrepresented the gift that the Lord had given him. Each lie has a consequence so let us see what happens this time!

Now because Abraham told this lie, the King of Gerar whose name was Abimelek, who noticed how beautiful she was told his men, "Hey, does anyone know who that fine queen is that just arrived in town? She came here with that rich man? If you do not know you had better ask somebody, find out who she is and bring her to me at once! I want to spend some quality time with her and maybe even take her for my wifey. Listen up, this is priority one. Find that shorty and bring her here to me at once!"

King Abimelek was feeling good about the prospect of meeting Sarah and spending time with her. He thought to himself, "We have some beautiful women here in Gerar, but none like her!! I can't wait!"

But God wasn't having this! He appeared to Abimelek in a dream shortly after he gave orders to his men. God spoke to him in this dream and said, "WAKE UP!! Do you not know that this woman, Sarah is married! If you do not return her to her husband at once, you will die! You can't have this married woman, not today or tomorrow! Return her at once!"

Now Abimelek had not had sex with Sarah or even gotten close enough to her to touch her, so he said, "Lord, I did not know, how can I be held accountable for something that I did not know? Will you destroy me, an innocent man who has nations in his seed! Did not Abraham say to me that, 'Sarah was his sister' and did she not back up Abraham's lie by saying that, 'Abraham was her brother?' I did not know and I acted with a clear mind, clean hands and with an innocent heart."

God replied, "I am well aware that you did not know and that you handled yourself with pure integrity; this is exactly why I am bringing this to YOUR attention. I have kept YOU from sinning against ME. Why do you think that you felt as though there was no rush in touching her or having sex with her? That was by my doing! Now, I want you to immediately give this married woman back to her husband! This man is my prophet, and I will have him to pray for you so that you will live and not die. Remember, that if you disobey me and keep the woman, you, everyone and everything connected to you will die. You can bet on that."

Earrrrrr-llllly the next morning, it was just before dawn, Abimelek wasn't playing around and was doing what he had to do, and that was to get Sarah back to Abraham. Abimelek called in all of his officials, and when he told them about what the Lord had revealed and told him, they were trembling with fear.

When they brought Abraham in Abimelek said, "What in all of heaven, earth, the moon and the stars have you done!? What did I do to you for you to bring the wrath of the Lord against me and mine?!! You knew better than this and knew that you and Sarah should not have told this bold face lie. The Lord said that you are His prophet, so being a prophet I know that the Lord showed you what would happen because of your lie, so you just didn't give a flip about me and mine!!"

And Abimelek asked Abraham, "Why would you do this!!? How could you rationalize this in your mind and heart? Aren't you supposed to be God's prophet?"

Abraham said, "Well, what had happened was I said to myself, these people do not fear God and I know that they will kill me and take my wife because she is such a beautiful queen. Well, in all actuality, it wasn't a complete lie, she really is my sister, and we have the same father but different mothers. She is my half-sister and because we weren't full blooded sister and brother I married her and she is my wife. And when God told me to leave my father's house and my hometown, I told her that if she loved me wherever we went she would say, 'That's my brother Abraham' Leaving my hometown and being out here on my own, with no family support or back up, I was scared for my life!"

When Abimelek heard this he felt sorry for him and thought that maybe he would show Abraham a little support even though he had been wronged. Abimelek had his men to bring Abraham some sheep and cattle, male and female slaves. Abimelek gave Abraham a prophet's reward, and he did not forget to give Sarah back to Abraham as the Lord told him to do. Abimelek thought that he would go a step further in making Abraham feel more at ease so he said, "All of Gerar is my kingdom. I invite you to choose any place that you like and live there for as long as you would like."

Abimelek then looked at Sarah and felt bad for her being used as a pawn by her own husband, because he wasn't man enough to stand strong and protect her, so he said to Sarah, "I am giving your brother a thousand shekels of silver because I know how people are going to look at you and how they are already talking about you."

One thousand Shekels of silver is equal to 25 pounds. One shekel equals $320.00 today, so Abimelek gave Abraham $8000.00 on Sarah's behalf. I know, you are probably asking the same question I asked, why didn't Abimelek give the money straight to Sarah since it's for her damages? Back in those days women had not rights, they were their husband's property and did not own anything.

Abimelek continued, "This is to cover the offense of what all of this foolishness, that your husband Abraham caused, looks like in the sight of others. Sarah, this will completely remove that stain from you and free you in their eyes."

After hearing this Abraham felt the urge to pray for Abimelek, and God sent down His healing power and released Abimelek, his wife and his female slaves from the curse that had fallen upon them. You see because of the lie that Abraham and Sarah told that made Abimelek take Sarah away from Abraham, the Lord caused a temporary curse to fall on all the women in Abimelek's household so that they could not get pregnant and have children.

Point(s) to Ponder: Why did Abraham and Sarah find it necessary to lie to King Abimelek the same way that they lied when they first came to Egypt in Genesis 12? Is lying and not trusting the Lord a pattern for Abraham and Sarah? Why was Abraham, again, so scared for his life and so willing to put Sarah, his wife, out there to others to protect himself? Why is more importance placed on Abraham giving Sarah to the king as being wrong and not Lot's daughters raping him?

Take Away: When the Lord sends us out to go to a particular place, He has already taken into consideration who and what we will encounter and He has our backs. We do not need to be like Abraham and Sarah and tell lies to cover our fear.

Prayer: Lord, we thank You today for Your instructions and guidance for our lives. We ask that our ears are opened to hear Your voice and that we are obedient to what You are saying. We trust You to not only direct us, but to protect us, for You are our strong tower and we run to You for safety.

Genesis 21: Pregnant at 90/100 yr. old huzband

Just as the Lord had previously told Abraham and Sarah, exactly a year later, Sarah became pregnant!! Abraham was 100 years old! Dude was up there, however old he was, Sarah finally became pregnant and had a son for Abraham and at the same time that God said it would happen! God's promises are true! The intimate pleasure that Sarah thought she was too old to enjoy became hers.

Abraham named the miracle baby Isaac, as the Lord told him to. Abraham remembered the agreement that he and the Lord made in Genesis 17 and he thought that he had better keep his end of the deal, so he circumcised the baby at 8 days old. Abraham was a powerful and youthful hundred years old when he got his wife Sarah pregnant and she had the miracle son. Wheeww chile, 100 years old!! Today, not many live to see 100 and here is Abraham still fertile and multiplying the earth!

Sarah got a kick out of this and said, "God has made me laugh again and I know that any and everyone who hears about me having this child at 90 years of age will also laugh! Who would've thunk that at 90 years old, I would be able to enjoy the pleasure of intimacy with my 100 year old husband, get pregnant, and have a child! All of this from a man who is 100 years old! I am sure that this is the talk of the camp! But that's alright, alright with me! Let everyone talk, I don't care what people say, because they now know that I have given Abraham a son at this old age and that all of this only happened by the hand of God!! Glory to God!"

The name Isaac means, 'He laughs.'

As Isaac grew and Sarah stopped breast feeding him, Abraham decided to have a house party to celebrate. Abraham was so caught up and marveling over his son Isaac that he did not notice what Ishmael was doing. Remember Ishmael, the son that Abraham had with his wife's servant named Hagar, well, he is back in the picture. Abraham didn't see what was happening to his miracle baby, but Mama Sarah saw it!! Yes, she did! Sarah didn't miss a thing. She saw that Ishmael was making fun of Isaac and calling him names. So Sarah said to Abraham, "Bae, you betta get yo gurl and her son, you betta get em!! I want her ANNNNNDUH her son gone! I want her and that boy away from my son, because now that we have an heir I want to make sure that, THAT woman's son, Ishmael, will never share in this. He doesn't deserve anything of yours!"

Now of course we would expect Sarah's words and vibrato to cause Abraham to get upset and anxious because Ishamel was also his son!! But God stepped in to quiet Abraham's spirit and said to him, "Do not worry about your son Ishmael and his mother Hagar. I want you to do whatever Sarah tells you to do, because just as I promised you, Isaac holds your legacy. BUT I will also do great things for Ishmael, your other son, just because he is your son! Great things will also come from him and his children, your grandchildren!"

After Abraham heard God's voice on the matter, he got up early the next morning and packed up a little bit of food and a little bit of water so that he could send Ishmael and Hagar away from him and Sarah, with at least a little something. Hagar side eyed Abraham and said, "So this is how you do the mother of your first son! I was there for you when that wife of yours couldn't give you a son and now that you have a son by her, you throw us away. WOW! With all of the riches that you have you, you send us out into the wilderness with a little bit of food and a little bit of water! Aren't you the generous and caring father! More like a deadbeat!"

After Hagar spoke her mind, she and Ishmael went on their way and ended up wandering in the Desert of Beersheba all alone. You would think that Abraham would have at least sent a servant with her and given her some livestock and money so that she could take care of herself and Ishmael, after all Abraham was a rich man and out of ALL of his riches, he felt that some food and water was good enough to survive the dessert and to have a good start after leaving his place. WOW, this is all that he gave the mother of his child to care for herself and his child!! Abraham could have done far better in his child support effort. You think?!

It didn't take long for Hagar and Ishmael to drink all of the water, especially since they ended up wandering around in the hot desert. Hagar was so sad and felt so helpless. She didn't know what to do so she placed Ishmael under one of the bushes, to try and protect him from the sun and heat, also because it broke her heart to hear him crying from thirst. She walked away from Ishmael and sat down a few feet away. She was very distressed and said to herself, "I just cannot watch my son die. What was Abraham thinking by sending us out her alone without any thing to live off of?

And with that she began to cry, a hard cry, from deep within her emotions. You know one of those cries where your stomach hurts, you can hardly catch your breath and snot and tears are all over your face. Yes, one of those "ugly face" cries.

Even though Hagar was crying loud, God still heard the cries of Ishmael! The angel of heaven said to her, "What's wrong Hagar? You no longer need to be scared and worried; God heard Ishmael crying from under the bush. Go back over to your son and pick him up from under the bush, take his little hand and know that greatness is his destiny, for I, the Lord will make him great."

And when God finished speaking those words, Hagar's eyes were open to what God had provided for her and Ishmael. Hagar was able to see a well filled with water, Hagar started crying again, shouting and thanking God. When she was done giving thanks she hurried over to the well and filled the container with water and gave the thirsty baby some water to drink.

From that day forward Hagar knew that Ishmael had favor in God's eyes and that God would always be with him. Hagar and Ishmael decided to live in the desert and Ishmael became an expert archer. Ishmael not only became an expert archer, but he also became a husband, because Hagar found him a fine Egyptian wife, with beautiful locks, copper skin tone and a gorgeous curvy body. This all took place in the Desert of Paran.

Ishamel was no longer crying under a bush, but shouting with joy because of his new BAE!!

Since Hagar and Ishmael left, things were great between Abraham and Sarah! They were prospering on all fronts. Abimelek and Phicol the commander noticed how good God was to Abraham, how Abraham was continually blessed by God, so they said to Abraham, "We have noticed that no matter what you do, God is with you! Now I need you to swear to me, right here before God, that you will treat me and my children and my descendants with fairness, decency and respect? You tricked me one time and almost got me and the entire city destroyed by God because you lied and said that Sarah was your sister and she even backed you up, so I need you to show me and this country, where you now live as a foreigner, the same kindness I have shown to you. Remember that I gave you animals and gave Sarah money, even though you both tricked me?"

Abraham could not deny this and had no other choice than to do what he was being asked of him, so he swore to Abimelek by saying, "I will treat you, your children and descendants fairly, decently and with respect and I will always be honest and upright towards you and yours."

Then Abraham thought that this was a great time to tell Abimelek what was going on and to ask him why his servants had stolen one of the wells of water that he dug? Abraham said, "Well, since we are talking and trying to be one hundred with each other, please tell me why your servants have taken possession of one of the wells that I dug for water?

Abimelek knew absolutely nothing about this and had not ordered this to happen so he said, "I haven't the slightest idea what you are talking about or who has done this. You're just telling me this NOW? Maybe, if I had heard about this earlier I could have taken care of it and it wouldn't be an issue. Bruh, why am I just hearing about the well today?"

Abraham thought to himself that maybe he should come up with a way to form an alliance with Abimelek so, he brought sheep and cattle and gave them to Abimelek. Abraham was a smart man and rather than go back and forth with Abimelek about the well and his men stealing it, he decided to give Abimelek some sheep, cattle, and to top it off he added in seven female sheep, probably some of the same sheep and cattle that Abimelek had given him for lying. Abraham thought that this make the treaty that much sweeter.

Abimelek thought that Abraham's actions were suspect so he asked, "Why have you separated the seven female sheep from the others?"

Abraham told Abimelek, "The seven female sheep are a gift for you and stand as a testament and witness that I dug this well! That this well belongs to me! Will you accept these as a gift and acknowledge that I dug this well?"

Abimelek accepted this as a sign that Abraham dug the well and the place where they swore their oath and treaty is called Beersheba. Beersheba means-well of oath.

After the treaty had been made at Beersheba, Abimelek and Phicol the commander, went back home. Their home is the same place the Philistines call home. On that same day, Abraham planted an evergreen tree in Beersheba, and there he called on the name of the LORD, the Eternal God. And the tree became a symbol so that all would know that Abraham would be staying in the hometown of the Philistines for a long time.

Points to ponder: Did Sarah have to throw Hagar and Ishmael out like that, after all she is the one who gave Hagar to Abraham to sleep with and have a child with? By throwing them out was Sarah trying to hide her mistake? Wasn't her son Isaac already guaranteed the inheritance whether Ishmael was around or not? Abraham was a rich man so why was he so stingy with what he gave Hagar and Ishamel? Did Abraham's stingy child support efforts set the stage for what is happening today; many father's not paying child support, not being in their child's lives and if they pay support it is only a small portion of what is needed for the child to survive?

Take Away: God is a man of His word. His promises are true and come to past in whatever time frame He sets. We just need to believe and wait patiently. We should not be like Sarah and try to do our own thing to make it happen. We should rather be about God's business as He attends to ours.

Prayer: Father we thank You today that Your promises to us are yes and Amen in You and that we can count on Your Word being performed in our lives and accomplishing the purpose that You send it to do. We ask You to give us the strength to stand on Your word to us, even in the face of opposition, adversity and our own fear.

Genesis 22: Abraham is acting "SUSPECT"

Sometime later after the Lord God blessed Sarah and Abraham with their son Isaac, God decided that He would test Abraham's faith in Him. We all witnessed how Sarah and Abraham laughed when they were told that they would have a child at their ripe old age, so God wanted to know just how far He could trust them to trust in Him.

God said to Abraham, "Abraham!"

Abraham answered, "Yes, Lord!"

This shows me that Abraham was used to hearing God's voice, because most today would be sceered and run off if they heard the audible voice of God. Be running down the street asking others, "Hey, did you hear that, did anyone else hear that? Am I losing it or maybe I had too much wine?"

Then God said to Abraham, "I need you to do something for me."

Abraham said, "Yes Lord, anything! You have given me my son Isaac, as you said you would, so name it, and I will do it."

God said, "Okay! I need you to take your son, Isaac, your only son that you and Sarah had together, the son that you love and go on a road trip to the region of Moriah. Once you get there, I am going to need you to sacrifice your son Isaac, as you would a lamb or any other burnt offering. I want you to do this on a mountain that I will show you once you two get there."

Abraham should have known that this was just a test because God previously told him, in Genesis 17, that He would confirm His covenant with Isaac and his descendants as an everlasting covenant. How quickly Abraham forgot.

All night long Abraham tossed and turned wondering how he would have the strength to sacrifice his only son, and even more he wondered what Sarah was going to do to him when she found out that he had sacrificed Isaac. He tossed and turned so much that Sarah asked him, "Abraham, honey, are you alright? Why are you so antsy and anxious tonight?"

Abraham replied, "I'm okay honey. I just have a lot on my mind, ya know I just want so much for our son, ya know?"

Sarah answered, "Yes, I do understand. He has a lot to learn and we have a lot to give him. Everything will be fine honey, now good night and be still, you're disturbing MY rest."

Abraham thought to himself, "What a selfish huzzy. You just do not know how disturbed your rest will be after I do what the Lord says and while I am at it, Lord how could you ask this of me? Why should I have to sacrifice my only son, I love you, but I don't want to burn my son. I guess as the saying goes, not my will Lord, but Your will be done, regardless of how I feel about it. Geesh, Lord isn't there anything else you could ask me to do?"

Abraham then turned over and tried his best to get some sleep, but his mind was racing like a horse at the thought of burning his son alive!! Regardless of how much his mind was racing, he knew he better be still in that bed and not wake Sarah!

Being the obedient man that he was, Abraham, got up early the next morning, loaded up his transport donkey, picked his best two servants to take with him and called to Isaac so that they could be on their way. Mt. Moriah was 55 miles away from where they lived. Five, 5, is the biblical number for Grace, so 55 miles, is double grace! God's grace was with Abraham and Isaac. Especially Isaac, he needed it the most.

Side note: Doesn't Mt Moriah sound like an old wooden Baptist church that sits off a dirt road out in the country? Well, anywho….

When Abraham had cut enough wood for the burnt offering, he set out for Mt Moriah, the place God told him about. On the third day Abraham was growing weary and worried even more about his assignment, but as he was walking and wondering he looked ahead and lo and behold he saw Mt. Moriah, the place that God said he would show him. Abraham said to his servants, "Watch over this donkey for me. I am going to take Isaac way over there and we will worship for a while and then we will be back."

Note: Abraham saw Mt Moriah on the third day. This is notable because it was on the third day that Jesus rose from the dead. Hmmmm…an interesting fact to take note of.

Abraham made Isaac carry the wood and he carried the fire and the knife. As the two of them went on together, Isaac thought that this entire situation seemed suspect, especially since he had seen his father make sacrificial offerings before, but this time there was no animal to sacrifice for the offering! Isaac began to wonder what was up with all of this! Isaac finally spoke up and said, "Er-Ummm, daddy?"

Abraham said, "Yes, my son?"

Isaac responded, "We have the fire and the wood, but where is the lamb for the burnt offering? Where's the animal?"

The closer they got to the altar location, the clearer Isaac wanted to be on the situation at hand! He was more than a little concerned about what was unfolding and kept giving Abraham the side eye.

Abraham thought to himself, "He is a smart one, nothing gets past him."

Abraham said to Isaac, "Sometimes Isaac, God provides the lamb for the burnt offering."

Isaac was still concerned, and growing more anxious by the second, but he accepted the answer, after all that was his father whom he knew loved him and would not harm him. So the two of them continued on together.

When they finally reached the place God had told Abraham about, Abraham set up an altar and placed the wood on it. He then looked at Isaac with very sad eyes, grabbed him before he could run away and then Abraham tied Isaac up and put him gently on top of the wood.

When Isaac found himself laying on top of the wood his worst fears had come alive and he said to himself, "I knew that I should have ran fast and far away from what daddy had going on. Did I not ask him where was the lamb for the burnt offering? Did he not give me that line about God providing!? If I get off this altar I bet I'll follow my mind next time and if I don't see a lamb I won't be the lamb!"

Isaac was surely crying out to God to save him, because at this point Isaac probably thought that his father had lost his mind. Isaac said, "Father what you are doing? God's people DO NOT sacrifice humans, let alone their own child!"

Isaac cried out real loud, "Lord please touch my daddy's mind and get me off this altar!"

At that moment while Isaac was crying out to the Lord, Abraham took out the knife and was about to kill his only son when the LORD called out to him all the way from heaven, "Abraham! Abraham!"

Abraham heard his name echoing and said with a sigh of relief, "Yes Lord, Yes Lord!!"

The Lord said, "Do NOT lay a hand on that boy, don't you do anything to him! Now that I have seen just how far you will you go to please me, you have passed the test and I know that you fear Me, because you were willing to kill your son just because I asked you to."

Chile, Isaac was rejoicing and thanking the Lord for hearing his cries, and stopping his father from killing him. If Isaac had not still been tied down to the altar he would have been dancing and shouting in a serious praise break!!

About this time Abraham looked away to wipe the tears and there in a thick part of the grass he saw a ram with the horns caught in something. Chile, Abraham ran over to the thick grass, grabbed that ram and he did not let the altar that he put together go to waste. He gladly sacrificed that ram instead of Isaac.

Isaac saw this and said to himself, "Now you see, if daddy had just waited a moment longer and not been in such a rush, the Lord would have provided the offering like he said. I knew that daddy or should I say Abraham, was doing TOO much when he put me up there on that altar! Wait til' I get home, I'm gone tell mama on him and he already knows she don't play when it comes to her precious miracle baby Isaac! ME! She don't play when it comes to me!!"

So Abraham said, "A good name for this spot is, "The LORD Will Provide."

You better know that with all of that drama and as Isaac told his mother and friends, this is still talked about and it is very often said, "On the mountain of the LORD it will be provided."

Many sermons have been preached even today about this with titles such as, "A ram in the bush,"; "Abraham done lost his mind,"; "Wait on God because He will provide,"; "Isaac CAN pray too" and my favorite, "Sarah whooped Abraham!"

After all of the commotion, God called to Abraham a second time, all the way from heaven and said, "I declare this day, because you have been obedient to My Word and went against everything that was in you not to kill your son, and placed him on the altar as a sacrifice just because I asked you to, I will most certainly bless you. I will bless you to have many offspring and to make them as plentiful as the stars on a starlit night and as bountiful as the sand on the beach. They will not be defeated but instead they will take over the cities of their enemies, and through your children everyone on earth will be blessed, all because you have pushed past your fear and feelings and obeyed Me."

Then Abraham and Isaac went back to where the servants were watching the transport donkey, and everyone went to Beersheba and Abraham decided to live in Beersheba. We still do not know why he did not want to go back to his beloved queen Sarah. Maybe Abraham was scared of what Sarah would do to him once she found out what happened at Mt. Moriah. We already know that Isaac is going to tell his mama Sarah and SARAH DON'T PLAY ABOUT HER MIRACLE BABY ISAAC!

After all of the Mt. Moriah drama had settled, Abraham received word from the street that Milkah, his brother's wife, was also a mother. She had given his brother Nahor EIGHT sons. Their names in the order of their birth were Uz and Buz (twins), Kemuel (who is known as the father of Aram), Kesed, Hazo, Pildash, Jidlaph and Bethuel. Wow, I think that we can all agree that these names are definitely different! Bethuel is Rebekah's father, who we will talk about a little later.

Milkah and Nahor were busy getting it on, how else would she have been able to have eight sons. It was as if Nahor was in a race with Abraham. Abraham had shared the conversation that he had with the Lord and how many children he would have, like the dust of the sand on the beach, so Nahor set out to get a head start. That brotherly competition was fierce! To add more salt on the wound, the word off the street was also that that Nahor's side chick, whose name was Reumah, also had 4 sons: Tebah, Gaham, Tahash and Maakah. That Nahor was a busy brutha!!

Abraham once again began to wonder if God's word would come to pass for him. He thought to himself, "What a head start Nahor has on me! I have only 2 sons, one from my wife and one from my side chick. He has 12 and I have 2. Dang! He already has a tribe!"

Point To Ponder: How frightening was the test of sacrifice for Isaac and Abraham? Isaac was the one on the altar, but Abraham knew that Sarah was going to have his head if he killed her miracle son! For a 100 and 90 year old to have a child was truly a miracle, shoot just for them to be able to be intimate was a miracle. You know Arthur and Ritis don't pay!

Take Away: How often has God tested us and because the sacrifice seemed to be too great we failed the test by not moving forward? Do you think that the gain of passing the test would have been that much greater than the sacrifice?

Prayer: Father we thank You today for the many life tests that You have given us and we ask for discernment to recognize them as tests. We further ask for the strength to be able to go through the test and complete it and no matter what the test requires of us we know that Your reward is greater.

Genesis 23: Sarah's passes away

Now it was a very sad day in Canaan, because Sarah, known her for her beauty, lived to be a hundred and twenty-seven years old before she went on to be with the Lord. The obituary read that she passed away while at Kiriath Arba (that is, Hebron) in the land of Canaan. It further read that Sarah made her transition to heaven without her husband Abraham at her side.

When Isaac told Abraham that Sarah had gone to be with the Lord, Abraham went from Beersheba to Hebron (31 miles) in the land of Canaan, to view her body, help Isaac with the home going service plans and of course he took time to mourn and cry over losing his beloved Sarah.

As much as Abraham and Sarah had gone through, it was hard to believe that he lived so far away from her and that he was not at her bedside when she passed away.

After shedding many tears of regret, Abraham wiped his eyes, rose from beside his dead wife to begin making the arrangements for Sarah's funeral. He went to talk with the Hittites and said, "You all know that I am not from here, I have been living in Beersheba, but my wife Sarah lived here for a long time. I am asking if you would please sell me some land so I can make a plot, right here, to bury my beloved deceased wife, Sarah."

Abraham didn't think that the Hittites knew who he was, but his reputation went before him and Sarah had told many about him, besides they saw him coming and going from Sarah's place in the middle of the night.

The Hittites said to Abraham, "Abraham, Abraham, we know who you are! We know that you are a powerful man of royalty, so please bury your wife. Choose which ever plot you would like and we will not deny you."

Again Abraham got up and this time he bowed low before the Hittites and said to them, "If you will let me bury my wife wherever I want then please go to Ephron, the son of Zohar, and plead my case, ya know, put in a good word for me so that he will let me buy, at whatever price he sets, the cave of Machpelah, which is at the backside of the field he owns. Please ask him to let me buy it. And as I said money is no object."

The Hittites were thinking to themselves, Ephron is sitting right there, why does this man not step up and ask Ephron for himself?

Ephron the Hittite WAS actually sitting right there in the crowd of people and heard every word that Abraham had spoken. Ephron said to Abraham, "Mighty man of God, be still and check this out; I will not sell you the land that you have asked about but instead I will GIVE it to you AND I will give you the cave because I remember your wife and how beautiful and kind she was. She would do anything for you and for Isaac. Her kindness did not stop there, she would help anyone in need. So to honor her and in her memory, right here in the presence of everyone, who are witnesses to all what I just said please take this gift and go setup up your wife's home going service."

Once again Abraham felt the need to bow down to the Hittites and Ephron and say, "I appreciate your gesture of kindness towards my wife, however I would rather pay full price for the field and cave. My Sarah is worth full price and more. So please let me pay the FULL price so I can go and bury my beloved Sarah there."

Ephron could feel what Abraham was saying and said, "Okay, okay. I understand what you are saying, Sarah is certainly worth full price and more! Alright then, the land is worth four hundred shekels of silver, ($128,000.00), but you and I are better than that, right? Go bury your wife."

Abraham did not want to owe Ephron anything and did not want a favor, he was not looking for a GoFundMe to bury his wife so Abraham agreed to pay Ephron the 400 hundred shekels of silver. Abraham weighed out the silver, right there on the spot, in front of everyone, so that they could be witnesses to the transaction.

So what used to be Ephron's field and cave in Machpelah near Mamre, and all the trees and everything that was on it, was sold and all the paperwork needed for Abraham to take possession of the property were completed and given to Abraham. The property was now his as he wished. All of this was done in the presence of all the Hittites who had heard on the news at 5 about Sarah's passing and came out to mourn her and pay their respects. After all of the legalities were over, and the all of the arrangements were done, Abraham buried his beloved deceased wife Sarah in the cave that he bought from Ephron. Sarah was laid to rest in the land of Canaan.

Points to Ponder: Why was Abraham living so far away from his wife Sarah? Why did Abraham not accept Ephron's offer and take the land and the cave for free? Did Ephron and the Hittites have a bad reputation for doing business?

Take Away: In all business dealings weigh the consequences, have witnesses and put it in a formal contract, especially when it is large amounts of money and property. Be sure that the person you are doing business with has integrity, no evil motive and is not just talking a good game.

Prayer: Lord we thank you for the wisdom and knowledge that comes from You as we conduct business on any level. We thank You for putting trustworthy people in our paths and for giving us Your wisdom and Your guidance as we not only conduct, but also in our daily lives.

Genesis 24: Isaac finds a wifey!

Abraham was old, grey and had bad eyes. He was reflecting and thinking about how good God had been to him and how God has blessed him with all that he needed and wanted. Abraham sent for the butler in charge of his house, the one in charge of all that he had and said, "I know that this is going to sound a little strange, but put your hand under my thigh."

This was the ancient way of saying that the servant is under Abraham's authority. The butler looked at Abraham with a frown, He had one eye brow up and the other down and wrinkles in the middle of his forehead. He thought to himself, "After all of these years, he knows that I don't play that!"

Abraham said to his butler in charge, "I want you to swear to me and to the LORD, that you will not find a bae, for my son Isaac, from amongst the females of the Canaanites, but instead I want you to go to my hometown, where all of my relatives are and get a wifey for Isaac from there."

The butler in charge said, "Wheew!! I thought you were going to ask me to do something else. But er um, YES, I will go as you have asked me to but I how can I expect a woman to come back with me? I don't expect the woman that I chose for Isaac to come back with me! With me! So, what if she does not want to come back with me to Canaan? What shall I do then? Should I come back to Canaan and get Isaac and take him to your hometown?"

When the butler asked if he should come back to Canaan and get Isaac and take him to Abraham's hometown that struck a nerve with Abraham. Abraham said, "What EVER you do, do NOT take my son there!"

Abraham wasn't playing about that thing and began to unpack the situation for the butler in charge. Abraham continued and said, "The LORD told me to leave my FATHER's household and to get out of my hometown. He also told me that He was going to give the land to my offspring. This is the same God that has sent one of His angels ahead to my hometown on your behalf. So go and get a wife for my son, the way is clear for you and the right lady is waiting for your arrival. Let's just say for your own peace of mind that the lady does not want to come back with you, then and only then will you be released from this assignment and can come back to me empty handed. BUT put this in the forefront of your mind, "DO NOT TAKE MY SON, ISAAC, BACK THERE! You got it?!"

So the butler in charge, reluctantly placed his right hand under Abraham's sweaty thigh and promised to do just as Abraham had told him to.

Shortly after the butler swore to Abraham that he would complete the assignment he left Canaan. The butler took ten of Abraham's camels which were loaded with all kinds of goods. The butler said to himself, "With all of this to offer the woman's father, how could they refuse?!"

The butler set the camel's GPS for Aram Naharaim and continued on to his destiny, which was the town of Nahor. According to the GPS this was a long journey of 400 miles with many twists and turns.

When the butler finally arrived it was in the evening time and he made the camels kneel down to rest near the well outside the town. In the evening time is when the women come out to the well to get water so the butler thought for sure he would see a beautiful woman for Isaac.

The butler did not want this to be a long and drawn out process especially since he had just travelled 400 miles to get there, so he prayed, "Lord God, I ask that You would make this be short and successful and if at all possible make it happen today. Please show me, the butler in charge of Abraham's house, some love and kindness. You see Lord, I am here standing beside the well where all of the women of the town come to get water, so to be sure that I have found the right woman for Isaac I ask that You would let everything go down like this; when I say to a young woman, 'Please give me some water from your jar?' and she will say, 'I guess it will be ok. You seem to be pretty decent, so here have some water and I will even give your camels some water.' Lord God please let her be the one that You want Isaac to be with. When all of this happens then and only then will I know in my heart that Isaac and Abraham will be pleased."

The butler in charge was very specific with his prayer and had developed a plan of how he would like all of this to happen. He created and placed that particular vision in his mind during the long trip there.

Before the butler had finished praying his specific and direct prayer to God, along comes beautiful Rebekah with her jar on her shoulder. Rebekah was the daughter of Bethuel son of Milkah. Remember Milkah in Genesis 22, Abraham's brother that was racing to have more children than Abraham, well, this is him. Nahor was the brother of Abraham, the brother that had eight sons by his wife and 4 more sons by his side chick.

Well, Rebekah was a very beautiful woman, and besides her beauty she was a virgin; no man had ever slept with her. Rebekah was waiting for the right man that would be her husband before she gave up the sweet cookies. She went down to the spring, filled her jar and came up again.

The butler saw her and thought, "WOW!! If I were not here for Isaac I would go after her for myself."

Upon seeing her the butler pulled himself together, tried to have some swag about himself and ran down to meet her. Once he was there, he thought that he had better say exactly would he had thought up and asked the Lord for, so he said, "Please give me some water from your jar."

Rebekah replied, "I guess it will be ok. You seem to be pretty decent, so here have some water and I will even give your camels some water."

And Rebekah quickly gave him some water to drink. After she had given him some water to drink, she said, "I will even give your camels some water."

The butler was overjoyed and began to dance in his heart, because the Lord heard his prayer and it went down just as he had asked and thought in his heart!!

The butler silently watched Rebekah. He actually watched her very closely because he was trying to find out more about the lady that the Lord had honored his prayer with. Even though the words were spoken, as the butler had asked of the Lord, he still wanted to see more.

The butler thought that this would be a great time to go into some of the goods that he had brought from Abraham and find something worthy of Rebekah's beauty. So when Rebekah finished watering the camels the butler in charge had a gold nose ring that weighed about a beka (1/2 ounce) and two gold bracelets that weighed ten shekels (11.34 grams). He felt as though if he gave these to her she would be more willing to talk to him, so he gave the gifts to her.

Then he asked her, "Who are your people? Who is your mother and father? I ask because I need a place to spend the night and prayerfully there is room in your father's house for me?"

Pause! Now we do know that times are certainly different. If a man walked up to a lady today and said what the butler said to Rebekah, what do you think would happen to him?! I'm just saying, who says that?!

Rebekah thought to herself, "Who is this man? First he asks for water and now he wants to know who my people are? This is a bit suspect!!"

Even though Rebekah had reservations she just couldn't resist answering the butler's questions. She answered the butler by saying, "My father's name is Bethuel. His father and mother's names are Milkah and Nahor; and I would say that we have plenty of straw and dry hay for the horses, and we will make sure that there is a room for you to comfortably spend the night."

The butler in charge was so excited that he took a quick bow to worship the LORD, broke out in a praise dance and said, "Praise the LORD, Praise Abraham's God, the God who has looked upon me with favor and kindness. God You have truly guided my feet as I made this trip for my master Abraham. You led me to my master's hometown and right to the relatives of my master!! What a mighty joyful day this is!!"

Rebekah ran back to her house as fast as she could and when she got there, chile, girlfriend told everyone about everything that was said and done at the well. She was so excited that the family had to tell her to slow down and breathe! She could hardly get it out.

Rebekah had a brother named Laban, and when he heard the story of what the butler in charge said to Rebekah his ears and eyes perked up when he saw the nose ring, and the bracelets on his sister's arms. Laban knew that he had to go and see who this man was. Laban said, "What is going on at the well!!"

So he ran with a quickness to the well to find out who this man was. Laban spoke to the butler and said, "What's up! Come on in! It seems that you are blessed and highly favored by the LORD! No need of standing out here by the well when we have prepared the house for you and a place for the camels to rest as well."

So the butler went with Laban to the house, and unloaded the camels. Straw and dry hay was already laid out for the camels to eat, and hot water with Epsom salt was brought in for the butler and his men to wash sand soak their feet. After they had had washed up and all the dust and dirt was gone from their feet, food was brought out and a feast was set down before them. Even though the butler and his men were starving and their stomachs were singing hunger tunes the butler said, "Thank you for the feast, but I can't eat until I tell you what's happening and why I am here! I will burst if I do not tell you why I am here. It is so very exciting how it all came together and worked out."

Laban said, "Well, alright, alright. If you must! Tell us what is up, ya know, whazz happenin'."

So the butler said, "I am Abraham's butler in charge. The LORD has blessed Abraham to be very wealthy. The Lord has given Abraham all kinds of livestock, precious metals like silver and gold, a full staff of male and female servants, and many transport camels and donkeys. At the age of 90, Abraham's wife Sarah gave him a son named Isaac. Can you believe it! Abraham was 100 years old! To make a long story short, in Abraham's will he is leaving everything that he owns to his son Isaac. Abraham wants his son to have a beautiful wife and not marry a Canaanite woman, so he made me swear to him that I would take a road trip to his hometown, find his family and find Isaac a beautiful wifey!"

The butler in charge continued, "So, I asked my master, what if I see the perfect woman for Isaac and she refuses to come back with me? I can't force her or kidnap her? Someone may report me thinking that I am into human trafficking or sex trafficking."

My master said to me, 'God has sent one of His angels ahead to my hometown on your behalf, so that you can get the absolute perfect woman to be a wife for Isaac from my own people, from my father's family. Now, if the woman refuses to return with you, then I will no longer hold you responsible for getting Isaac a wife, because it is out of your hands.'

The butler continued, "So I came here as instructed and when I arrived at the spring today I prayed, 'LORD, God of my master Abraham, if you will PLEASE let the right woman come along so that I can find a wife for Isaac and I would not have come all this way for nothing. Lord, please as I am standing beside this spring, let a young beautiful woman come to the well and when she does I will say to her, "May I have some water from your jar?" and if she says, 'I guess it will be ok. You seem to be pretty decent, so here have some water and I will even give your camels some water.' Father God, I ask that she would be the one."

The butler joyfully shouted, "And ain't it just like GOD!! Ha-le-luuuu-jah!! Before I was even finished praying what was in my heart, along comes Rebekah, with her jar on her shoulder and her beauty radiating in the sun of the day. She went down to the spring to get water, and I spoke to her and said, 'May I have some water from your jar.' "And with a quickness, she lowered the jar from her shoulder and said, 'I guess it will be ok. You seem to be pretty decent, so here have some water and I will even give your camels some water."

The butler was very expressive when he said, "I was so astonished! Ya know, that this all happened just as I had prayed it and visualized it would. I was amazed at how God moved, so I asked her, whose daughter are you? Who are your people?"

Then Rebekah said, "My father's name is Bethuel, who is the son of my grandfather Nahor, and Milkah, my grandmother."

The butler said, "When I heard this, I remembered the gifts that I had from my master Abraham. I brought these along just in case I found the right woman for Isaac, I wanted to be able to impress her. So I got the gifts out and I put the gold ring in her nose and the gold bracelets on her arms!"

He continued, "And because I was so overwhelmed by what God had done and provided I bowed down and worshiped the LORD. I began to walk back and forth and clap my hands as I ba-roke out in a praise to the LORD, the God of my master Abraham, who had led me RIGHT to the place to get the granddaughter of my master's brother for his son. Even as I tell you the story, I feel my Help coming on!!

After the butler came down from praise mode he said, "Now if you, Rebekah, are willing to come with me and if you, her family, are willing to let her go with me please let me know so that I will know what to do next?"

Laban and Bethuel had a short meeting and then said in a very deep voice to show authority, "We have determined that what has taken place is truly something that only God could do, so Rebekah will be happy to go with you and we are happy to let her go, because we know the Lord has directed all of this."

When the butler heard this he once again bowed down to the ground before the LORD!! Then he got up went into the bag with gifts once again and brought out the gold and silver jewelry and some designer clothing and gave them to Rebekah. He felt so great about the entire situation that he even gave expensive gifts to her brother and to her mother. Then he and the men who were with him ate, drank and spent the night there.

Rebekah's family talked all night long saying, "The Lord has really sent a good one this way for Rebekah! Look at all of the gifts that he has not only given to her, but to us also!! She has got a good one, she won't be hurtin for nothing! I think that we should play this to our advantage, let's come up with a plan!"

When the butler and his crew got up the next morning, he said, "We thank you for feeding the camels and letting us crash here last night, but it is time for us to take the long trip back."

But Rebekah's brother and mother said, "We talked and decided that Rebekah will stay with us for ten-ish days or so; then maybe you can leave."

The Butler didn't like this, because he had been very generous to them all and they had finalized everything the night before. He did not and could not understand what was going on. What kind of scam were they trying to run on him! The butler said with great vibrato and a seriously frowned face, "What in the world are you trying to do? DO NOT play games with me. DO NOT hold me up and certainly don't you try and play me! It was just last night that you, yourselves said that this was all directed by the Lord, so how can you stand in GOD'S way?! Let us go, NOW!"

At this point they thought and said to each other, "Wow! Well I guess we did not see that coming. We certainly did not expect him to swing things to the left and get so upset about staying a few more days."

So they called in Rebekah and asked her, "Do you reeeaaalllly want to go with this man?"

Rebekah said while rolling her eyes and raising her eyebrows, "Do you reeeaaalllly need to ask me that? YASSS and most certainly I will go with this man!"

Rebekah thought to herself, "There are no good prospects for a husband around here and I am so ready to get outta here and away from you controlling people, I would have left if he asked me at the well."

So with Rebekah's answer and seeing her demeanor and facial expressions they said, "Okay, she can go now and take her nurse with her."

And they also blessed Rebekah with spoken word by saying, "Our sister and daughter, may the Lord our God provide you with all that you need and more. May you have an abundance of children and may your children be strong and smart and take the cities of their enemies."

After the spoken word performance was over, Rebekah and her attendants including the nurse, got ready and mounted the camels and went back with the butler and his crew.

While they were on their journey, Rebekah confided in her nurse, "I certainly pray that I did not make a mistake by coming with this man and I most definitely hope that this Isaac person is a fine and well-endowed man, ya know, with a six pack and all that!! Gurl, may the Lord truly bless ME!!"

Back at Abraham's spot, Isaac had come from Beer Lahai Roi back to the Negev where he was staying. Late one evening Isaac went out to the field to meditate and pray, because he knew what his father had sent the butler in charge to do. Isaac prayed, "Lord let the woman that our butler finds for me be beautiful, have a kind and sweet heart, have beautiful locks in her hair and have a voluptuous body."

Just as he completed his prayer he looked up and saw the camels and the transport donkeys coming down the road. And as God would have it, Rebekah looked up and saw Isaac. Their eyes locked upon each other and Rebekah jumped off that camel, ran to the butler and said to him, "WOW! Wow! Wow! Who is THAT man in the field coming to meet us? Is that Isaac?"

The butler smiled real hard to keep from laughing out loud and said, "Yes, my sister, that is Master Isaac, the one that I have been telling you about!"

With that Rebekah decided that she would play shy, so she took her veil and covered her face. I don't know why she tried that because Isaac had seen her just as she saw him. That's why he was running to meet them.

Once Isaac reached them, the butler began to tell Isaac the story of all that had transpired.

Isaac was surely pleased with what the butler in charge had done and more importantly with how beautiful Rebekah was and how God had so quickly answered his prayer.

Isaac was like, "Yeah, yeah, now who is this woman with you?"

The butler answered, "This is your bae! Your soon to be wifey, Rebekah!"

Isaac was so beside himself and delighted that he immediately took Rebekah to his mama, Sarah's tent. Chile now you know Rebekah was special, Isaac took her to his mama's tent. Isaac had that tent set up like a memorial to his mother since she had passed away. The tent was very special to Isaac.

Both Rebekah and Isaac were beside themselves with how God had answered their prayers. Isaac was fine, well-endowed and had a six pack and all that and Rebekah was beautiful, with a kind and sweetheart, had beautiful locks in her hair and a voluptuous body. Isaac married Rebekah and she happily became his wife. Isaac looovveedd Rebekah and found the joy, intimacy and comfort in Rebekah that he needed to help him get through the death of his mother, Sarah.

Point to Ponder: Why did Laban and Nahor so quickly accept the Butler's story and agree to let Rebekah go? Why did they try to change the deal and ask for another 10 days?

Take away: We can witness the power of God and how He fulfilled His promise to Abraham when the Butler found favor in completing his task. The prayers that the Butler, Rebekah and Isaac prayed were fulfilled as a part of the promise that God had made to Abraham. When we pray into what God has promised us and not our will above His will, God, as witnessed in this passage, will move on our behalf.

Prayer: Father we thank You today for Your promises to us. We pray now, according to Your will for us and wait patiently for You to move on our behalf. We understand that You may not always move as WE want, but that You will move according to Your plan and promise for our life.

Genesis 25: Abraham goes home to be with the Lord.

After the death of Sarah, Abraham was so used to being with someone that he did not want to be alone. He thought to himself, "I am just too old to be in this world alone by myself so I believe that I will find me another bae."

It didn't take Abraham long time to get him a bed warmer, after all he was a rich man and the women had been lined up and waiting to get his attention ever since before Sarah passed.

Abraham found another wife named Keturah. Keturah was VERY fertile and gave Abraham six sons named Zimran, Jokshan, Medan, Midian, Ishbak and Shuah. And the sons gave Abraham and Keturah plenty of grandchildren. Jokshan was the father of Sheba and Dedan and the descendants of Dedan were the Ashurites, the Letushites and the Leummites. The sons of Midian were Ephah, Epher, Hanok, Abida and Eldaah. All of these were the bloodline of Keturah.

Abraham honored his son Isaac as the first and only son that he had with his deceased wife Sarah and in his will he left everything he owned to Isaac. Abraham was not heartless and learned not to be stingy towards his other sons, like he had been with Ishmael, because before he died he made sure that he gave all of them gifts and moved them "away" from Isaac, to the land of the east.

Abraham had not forgotten how ill-mannered and disrespectful Ishmael was at the house party he threw for his son Isaac, but as he thought about it he began to understand Ishmael's anger issues. He also remembered what Sarah said about Ishamel and why she wanted him away from Isaac. In Sarah's eyes Ishmael was a bad seed, but at this age Abraham felt guilty about the way he sent Hagar and Ishmael away with nothing, so he was trying hard to make things better before he left this earth.

Abraham was blessed with a long life and lived to be one hundred and seventy-five! When Abraham breathed his last breath and died he was an old man who had lived a full and exciting life. Many gathered to mourn and pay their respect to him and his family. Many came from near and far to attend his home going service and burial.

Abraham's sons, Isaac and Ishmael, made sure that Abraham was buried in the cave of Machpelah near Mamre, right next to his true beloved Sarah. Keturah, Abraham's last wife, was a little upset by that move, but there wasn't anything that she could do about it. Keturah was overheard saying, "I wanted to be buried next to my man. Even in death, he still idolizes Sarah."

After Abraham's death the Lord began to release many blessings upon Isaac. There were so many blessings that they fell like rain upon Isaac's head. At this time Isaac was living near Beer Lahai Roi.

Yes, Isaac was being blessed, but let us not forget about Ishmael. Remember him, the son that Abraham had with Sarah's servant Hagar the Egyptian, the one that Abraham sent away with some food and some water? Well, he had a lot of children and they are listed below.

Ishmael had 12 sons and their names, from oldest to youngest, are: Nebaioth, Kedar, Adbeel, Mibsam, Mishma, Dumah, Massa, Hadad, Tema, Jetur, Naphish and

Kedemah. These were the 12 sons of Ishmael, who became twelve tribal rulers. Ishmael lived to be one hundred and thirty-seven years of age. When Ishmael went on to be with the Lord, all of his people gathered to mourn and to attend his home going service.

Ishmael's bloodline decided to settle somewhere around Havilah to Shur, near the eastern border of Egypt, as you go toward Ashur. And not one of them got along with the other. They all had an issue with each other and whoever was related to them. It was always some drama, stress and strife going in their camps. We do not know how many times five-0 was called out to stop the insanity. They were like others we know, won't let you enjoy a holiday or have fun without causing enough trouble to leave somebody mad and not speaking or just enough to have somebody arrested, due to their foolishness.

Why were they like this? Remember what the Lord told Hagar in Genesis 16:12, "Ishmael will be a wild donkey of a man; he will not get along with anyone. He will think that everyone's against him and he will never get along with any of his relatives."

It looks as if Ishmael's spirit of hostility is something that he passed down through his bloodline. That is some kind of nasty "Generational curse!"

Ishmael was not the only one who had been fruitful and multiplying, Isaac was most certainly about that married life.

Just a recap, Abraham became the father of Isaac at 100 years old, and Isaac was forty years old when he married Rebekah daughter of Bethuel the Aramean from Paddan Aram and sister of Laban the Aramean. That's right, Isaac married his cousin!! Cousin wife, cousin husband. Cousin couple!

Isaac prayed to the LORD, because Rebekah was like his mother Sarah, she was unable to have chiren. Isaac remembered the story that his father Abraham told him about his mother Sarah being unable to have children and how the Lord blessed her at an old age to have him, but Isaac did not want to wait until he was 100 and his wife Rebekah was 90, so Isaac prayed one of those fire spittin' prayers, full of passion and commitment and he also understood that faith without works is dead, so he and Rebekah practiced the art of baby making on a REGULAR to reinforce his prayers and BEHOLD, The LORD answered his prayer!! Yes, sirrrr, Rebekah became pregnant! Isaac did his thing! He was determined not to wait another 60 years for a child.

Rebekah was not only pregnant but she was carrying twins!! The two babies wrestled and fought each other, day and night, even while they were in Rebekah's stomach! It was so much rumbling in her belly that Rebekah had to ask the Lord, "WHY?! Why is this happening to me? What is wrong with these babies? Why do they move about in my stomach so violently?"

The LORD said to her, "Rebekah, my daughter, this has to be because these babies represent two NATIONS. Two nations are in your stomach, not just babies, but NATIONS!! Nations are always at war. These two that are inside of you will not get along at all. One will be stronger than the other and the one that is born first will be under the foot of the younger one."

Rebekah meditated on this Word the Lord had given her and said to herself, "This is very powerful! I am carrying TWO NATIONS inside of me! WOW!"

When Labor Day came for Rebekah and the twins, she had boys! The oldest one came out first and was as red as the sunset! He had hair all over his tiny little body. Believe me, not one place on his body was without hair and because he was so red and hairy they named him Esau. Esau was also called Edom which means Red.

Shortly after Esau was born, his brother came out, and when he came out everyone was amazed because he had a strong firm grip on Esau's heel and because of this he was name Jacob. When the twins were born Isaac was sixty years old.

As the twins grew up Esau became an expert hunter. He loved being outside in the elements of the sun, wind, rain and anything that nature had to offer. Maybe because he was so hairy it was always too hot for him indoors. On the other hand Jacob was a home body and was very happy being in the house. Isaac loved himself some wild game and Esau was his favorite of the twins, while Rebekah favored Jacob.

One day Jacob was in the kitchen cooking some stew and Esau came in from hunting and was hungrier than a bear. The first thing that Jacob said was, "Esau! Dude, you smell like outdoors, go do something about that, PLEASE!"

But Esau could only think of how hungry he was and said to Jacob, "Quick, let me have some of that red stew before I pass out! Bruh, I have been out there hunting and chasing animals all day! Where do you think the meat for that stew came from? It came from my hard work, now GIVE ME SOME STEW!! I'm too hungry!"

Jacob thought to himself, I am going to see just how hungry he really is and said, "If you want some of THIS stew I will need something from you."

Esau said, "Sure, anything, just name it and it's yours."

Esau did not consider how crafty his brother Jacob had become. He had his mama Rebekah's wit and scheming mindset.

Jacob came back at Esau and said, "I will need you to give me your birthright (inheritance) and then I will give you some stew. I want everything that daddy is planning on leaving you in his will!"

Esau was shocked by what Jacob had said to him and said "What in all of heaven, earth, the sun, stars and the moon are you asking? Bruh, really! Look, I am about to die of hunger and you are trying to take me for what is rightfully mine. I can't help it because I came out of mom's stomach first. That's on you!!"

But then Esau begin to think differently as he grew weaker and hungrier and the stomach pains and growling increased. He thought about it and said, "What good is the birthright to me if I die of starvation? It's yours."

Jacob thought, boy I got him now, just where I want him!! Jacob said, "Swear to me first that you will give your birthright for some of this red stew? Swear it!"

So Esau swore an oath to Jacob and sold his birthright as first son to Jacob for some stew. Wow, that con-artist Jacob was sum-ting else!

With this the word that the Lord had spoken to Rebekah came to pass, "The one that is born first will serve the younger one."

Since the deal was sealed, Jacob gave Esau some bread and some of the Red stew with lentils in it. Esau was happier than a lark and ate and drank until his heart was content. Then Esau got up from the table and left. He left and began to think about what his own brother, Jacob, had done to him just because he was hungry! He became angrier and felt some kind of way towards Jacob. He thought to himself, "My own brother! How low down and dirty can you get? He scammed me right out of my God given birthright!"

Esau was really red now, red from anger. From that day on Esau despised his birthright because his brother Jacob now owned it.

You probably ask why is this birthright so important? Well, just like with Abraham and Isaac, when Abraham died Isaac inherited all of Abraham's possession, wealth and status. Esau, for a bowl of red stew, gave all of that up.

Point to Ponder: Why was Jacob so determined to get Esau's birthright and why did he use trickery to do so? Was this something that he thought up on his own or did Rebekah play a part in this? Could Esau have gotten something else to ease his hunger? Could he have just moved Jacob out of the way and fixed his own bread and soup?

Take Away: Don't let temporary measures or temporary fixes cause you to lose your right to a future inheritance. Don't let temporary situations cause you to lose focus on important matters that if neglected will cost you your future.

Prayer: Father we thank You today for the inheritance of a future with You. We ask that You would keep us focused on You and not let the temporary situations in this world, that we will face, draw us away from You.

Genesis 26: Isaac – A Liar like his Father

Do you remember King Abimelek from Genesis 20? This is the king that Abraham and Sarah lied to about being brother and sister. Well, he is back in the picture again. Just like in Abraham's time, another famine came to the land and Isaac went to see King Abimelek, the king of the Philistines in Gerar.

However, before Isaac went, the LORD appeared to Isaac and said, "ISAAC, ISAAC!! Listen up and listen carefully. I Do NOT want you and your family to go to Egypt; DON'T YOU DO IT! I want you to live in the land where **"I"** say live. Pitch a tent right here in this place until I tell you to leave. Now, be obedient to me and do what I say and I will always be by your side and of course you know that I will continually bless you. I will give all this land to you and yours and will keep the agreement that I had with your father Abraham. You will have so many children and such a big family line that it will be just as beautiful and plentiful as stars on a starlit night and because you will have so many children, they will bless many here on earth. I will do this for you because of your father! Abraham listened to Me and even when I gave him hard tasks, things that were unusual and out of the ordinary, he still did it!"

After hearing what the Lord said to him, Isaac thought it might just be best to stay put in the city of Gerar. He did not think that he had a need to go elsewhere since the Lord said He would be with him, give him the land and bless him with many children. Isaac thought to himself, "What more can a man want? Ya know! Hey, it doesn't get any better than this!"

When the Philistine men asked Isaac about Rebekah, just like his father Abraham had lied when he was asked about his wife Sarah, Isaac lied! Abraham lied twice about Sarah and said, 'She is my sister' and here comes Isaac doing the same thing!

JUST like his father Abraham, Isaac repeated the exact lie, using the same exact phrase for the same exact reason! He was scared to say that Rebekah was his wife, thinking that the Philistines would kill him and take Rebekah, because she is so beautiful.

Was this lie and fear generational? Was this passed down to Isaac in the bloodline from his father Abraham? Isaac wasn't even born when Abraham lied so how would he be able to repeat the same exact words for the same exact reason? More importantly will Isaac pass this down to his sons or will it stop right here and now?

Okay, back to the story at hand! Gotta see what's going to happen!

One of the worse things a person can do is to become too comfortable with the lie (s) they have told. That's what happened to Isaac! After a while Isaac became comfortable and forgot that Rebekah was supposed to be his sister. Isaac became relaxed and one day, King Abimelek was looking out of his window to glance over his kingdom and bay-bay, he saw Isaac pushing up all over Rebekah, like a husband does his wife!! Isaac was kissing all over her neck and back and Rebekah was obviously enjoying it. Abimelek had a flash back from Abraham and Sarah and told his men, "Go and get that lying buzzard Isaac and bring him and that heifer Rebekah to my chambers immediately!"

His men went and got Isaac and placed him in front of Abimelek. You would think that Isaac would have been humble, because he was being brought to the king in a hostile manner. It didn't seem to register on Isaac's mind that his lie might have been discovered. Isaac said, "What is the meaning of this? I was very busy when your men interrupted me! What could be so very important?!"

Abimelek said, "Yeah, I saw just how busy you were and what you were doing! How dare you question me! I have been very kind and generous to you, because of your father Abraham, but I now know that you and your father Abraham are just a like! You most certainly are your father Abraham's son!"

Isaac thought Abimelek was about to say something good and pay him a compliment and said, "Well thank you, but you didn't have to bring me here, right now to tell me this. Couldn't this have waited? As I said I was very busy!"

Abimelek gave Isaac the side eye and said, "I saw you pushing up on Rebekah! YES!! You were all over her! Is that how you treat your SISTA?! Tell the truth, who is she really to you? Is she your side chick or really your wife?"

One of Abimelek's men was ear hustling (that seemed to be the thing in this time period since they didn't have cell phones or spy cameras back then) and said to his buddy, "Dude, the King is ripping Isaac apart. I guess he saw Isaac pushing up all over his sister kissing and carrying on!! This is getting good, you should come and listen with me?"

The other guard said, "Naw, uh-uh! Man that's all you! If you get caught you do know that the King will have your head on a platter! You go right ahead, but if you don't get caught I want all of the details!"

King Abimelek said to Isaac, "Why did you say, 'She is my sister?' Why did you lie just LIKE your father, using the same exact words? Does this lying spirit run in your family?! It must, because this is the same EXACT lie that your father told me!!"

Isaac looked shocked, blindsided and caught off guard! With a broken voice Isaac said, "You see, your grace, King Abimelek, what had happened was that I thought I would be killed. My wife, Rebekah is so beautiful, I thought that someone would take her and kill me."

Then Abimelek became even more pissed off and got right in Isaac's face and said, "What is wrong with you? What were you thinking? Why have you have done this to us? Just, what if one of my men, or even me, would have slept with her, then what? Let me tell you what! That would have been adultery and the Lord would have rained HIS punishment and wrath down upon us because of YOUR lie!!"

So Abimelek gave orders to all the people saying, "Anyone who harms this man Isaac or Rebekah, his wife, I will personally see to it that they are killed, deaded, put to death however I see fit."

After this altercation Isaac began to think about all that was said and how could he have done the same exact thing as his father did and to the same king? He was baffled and puzzled and was deeply disturbed by what he had done.

King Abimelek told Isaac, "Get out of my presence and if I hear of or SEE any more of your foolery I won't be so forgiving next time."

Isaac ran out of the palace with a quickness and thought to himself, "I can't wait to see my baby Rebekah! Now we don't have to hide anymore! If the King knows who we are, everyone else knows who we are and we can be public!"

So Isaac rushed home to his wifey and they enjoyed each other's company the rest of that day.

Now that all of that was cleared up Isaac went on to plant some crops that same year and when the harvest came in from the crops, Isaac couldn't believe it! The crop gave him a hundred percent increase and this happened because the LORD saw fit to bless Isaac! Isaac became rich, his wealth continued to grow and he became one of the elites of Gerar due to his wealth. He had so many flocks and herds of animals and so many servants that the Philistines became jealous. One Philistine was overheard saying, "If King Abimelek had not said that he would kill anyone that harms Isaac or his wife, I swear, I would pull up on Isaac, take his wife and his possessions. Who does he think he is coming into our land and getting rich off of our resources? And then, and THEN to top it off he flosses around here like he is the king!"

The Philistines became very vindictive and felt as though they just had to do something about Isaac, even though they could not harm Isaac physically they came up with a way to ease their jealousy and to get back at Isaac. They held a meeting and came up with a plan. One of the men said, "I got it, I got it! You know all of the wells that

Isaac's father Abraham had his servants to dig on our land, what if we filled them all with dirt? That would slow his roll and make him rethink who he is and who's land he is on!"

All of the other Philistines in the meeting agreed and thought that was a great plan to humble Isaac, so the Philistines filled all those wells with dirt! Thy thought that surely this would cause Isaac to leave.

It seems that the spirit of jealousy attacked Abimelek as well, because he ordered Isaac to move away from him and his people, saying, "You know that man Isaac has become too powerful. He walks around MY kingdom giving orders and acting like he's in charge. Besides being a liar, like his daddy, he is also an arrogant prick!! I want him out of here, away from my people and MY kingdom once and for all. RIGHT NOW!! GET HIM OUT OF MY KINGDOM!!"

King Abimelek thought that he should deliver the news to Isaac so he said, "I been seeing you and noticing you! You are doing way too much on my land. You have become too rich, too powerful and I am demanding that you get all of your possessions, all of your people and whatever else that you have around here and get out immediately! You have been served a royal eviction notice and you do not have thirty days to vacate. I will give you a few hours to leave!"

This meant that Isaac's wealth and possession were becoming so great that King Abimelek felt intimidated. So Isaac had no choice but to move. He gathered all of his possessions and people and went down to the Valley of Gerar and decided to stay there.

Isaac thought to himself and spoke it out loud, "These Philistines just do not know who they are dealing with! They had better recognize the hand of God on my life and if they can't see it for themselves, they betta ask SOME-body!"

After the rushed move, Isaac had his men to unpack and start working quickly on removing the dirt from the wells that his father Abraham had dug. He also named the wells the same names that his father had given them.

Isaac told his servants, "Dig in other places in the valley and you will find other wells."

And when they did as Isaac said they discovered a fresh water well! Of course, the shepherds in the area were upset because they felt as though Isaac was an outsider and he came into their land and dug a well without their permission. They began to fight and argue with Isaac saying, "That's our water! We don't care if you did dig it! You didn't ask us first. We see why King Abimelek kicked you out of his kingdom. You have that "Take-over" spirit like your father."

Isaac paid them no attention and told his men, "Name that fresh water well Esek, because these people continue to argue and come for me. And while you are at it dig another well."

So Isaac's men dug another well and the people of the land argued with him again over THIS well, so he named it Sitnah. All of this arguing and the people taking the wells was becoming a pain in Isaac's plans and because of the argumentative, ungrateful, greedy and stingy people in the land, Isaac moved on and dug another well, and this time no one came for him about the well. So with this well Isaac said to his people, "Name this well Rehoboth, because the LORD has seen our struggle and found a place in this land for us and because He has we will now grow and increase again!"

Isaac started expanding and moved from the Valley of Gerar to Beersheba. On the same night of the move the LORD came to Isaac and said, "Isaac, now you know me just as your father Abraham knew me. You do not have to walk in fear and be scared, because I will always be with you, right by your side and leading the way. I will continue to shower you with blessings and your family will also get bigger, with more children. I will do all of this for you because of your father Abraham."

After the Lord spoke to Isaac he felt a bit more safe and comfortable in his heart and mind and for his family because God was with him. Isaac thought that he should make an altar in that very spot where the Lord spoke to him on a personal level. After the altar was complete, Isaac went in to a heavy and deep time of worship, for the Lord had been so good to him. After spending time with the Lord Isaac decided to stay there for a while, so he had the servants to put up his tent and also to dig another well.

What happens next is almost unbelievable. You cannot fathom what is about to take place!

Can you believe that after throwing Isaac and his people out of his kingdom and telling them to 'get out now', that Abimelek, yes King Abimelek, came from Gerar with Ahuzzath his personal adviser and Phicol the commander of his forces to personally see Isaac! Say Whatt!!

When Isaac saw them coming he said to himself and his staff, "I know that this can only be trouble! What does he want now? He threw us out, let his people take all of the wells that we dug and now he pulls up and shows his face here, today! That's a bold move!"

Isaac was very apprehensive about this visit, especially since they did not part on good terms. Isaac asked Abimelek, "Why are you here? Why have you come to see me?! Do you remember how hateful and hostile you were to me and mine? Have you forgotten how you threw us out and told us to move away from you, NOW? Not to mention how you allowed your people to take our wells, even the wells my father Abraham dug, that had been there for years! What do you want?"

Abimelek and his crew knew that Isaac was right and answered, "We regret what we did to you and how we treated you. It is now, that we can clearly see that the LORD is with you. We talked about it and decided that we should have an agreement with you. You know, there should be a sworn agreement between us, you know what I mean, like a treaty? We think that the treaty will make us feel safer and would let us know, beyond a shadow of a doubt, that you will not harm us! Remember when you were in my kingdom, even when you lied to me, I did not harm you and before that I always treated you like family. As I remember, I even sent you away peacefully. NOW you are blessed by the LORD. How does this treaty sound to you?"

Isaac thought that this was pretty "Philistine" decent of them, and said to himself, "King Abimelek is really intimidated and fearful of me. I wonder who told him that he had better recognize that the hand of the Lord was upon my life. I did say that he betta ask SOME-body, maybe he did."

After thinking it over, Isaac agreed to the treaty and even decided to have a good old fashion barbecue for them. They partied hard that night with plenty to eat and drink. Early the next morning before Abimelek and his crew departed they all agreed on what the treaty should say, signed it and even verbally swore an to each other. After this they peacefully went away. Isn't this the same thing that Abimelek had Abraham swear to him?

On that very day Isaac's servants came and told him, "Sir, it is fantastic how God is blessing us. Today we dug a well and fresh water is spouting out of it!!"

So Isaac named the well Shibah, and the town that it is in is still called Beersheba. Seems like all things are going well for Isaac, so let's briefly check in on Esau before we move on.

Now Esau had matured greatly and was a good strong forty years of age. He also found him a wifey and her name was Judith (an unusual bible name). Judith's father was Beeri and he was a Hittite. Esau was a bit greedy and decided he wanted a second wife and her name was Basemath. Her father's name was Elon and he was a Hittite. Judith and her family did not get along with Isaac's wife Rebekah. They were a constant source of drama. Man, they always had something negative to say. They wanted to be like the Joneses and were constantly doing way too much. Their actions caused Isaac and

Rebekah to have many sleepless nights because they were stressed out. We will discover why they were a source of grief to Isaac and Rebekah a bit later.

Point to Ponder: Was Isaac's lying a generational curse? He displayed the same behaviors and even spoke the same exact words as his father and he lied for the same exact reason his father Abraham lied? What was it that made King Abimelek want to form a treaty with Isaac? Was this a set up for something to come in the future?

Take Away: Instead of taking on the same negative aspects of our family, let us break those curses off of our lives and out of our family's bloodline. With this our children and their children will not have to deal with those negative and damaging generational behaviors.

Prayer: Father we thank You today for giving us insight into what a generational curse looks like and how it affects us and our bloodline. We ask, in the name of Your son Yeshua, that You would give us the ability to recognize things for what they are and the strength to respond, cut it at its roots and out of our blood line so that we can live productive, healthy and abundant lives in You.

Genesis 27: Ear Hustler Scams OG Isaac!

Now Isaac was an old man and apparently he had either cataracts or glaucoma, because his eyes were very blurry and he could hardly see anything. He was considered to be legally blind and wasn't allowed to drive anymore. Anywho, Isaac sent for Esau, his firstborn twin, to come and talk to him.

Esau came in and announced that he was there, because he knew that his father could not see him. Esau said, "Yes, father, I am here. You wanted to talk to me?"

Isaac said, "Yes, son. I am glad that you came in from the fields to talk to and see your old dad! Son, as you can see I am up there in age and honestly the way that my body feels I do not know how much longer I'll be around, so I need you to do something for me before I leave this earth and because I feel so bad in my body I need you to do it today for me, okay?"

Esau said, "Daddy don't talk like that now. I am sure that the Lord will give you many more years here with us and yes, anything that you want."

Isaac said, "Please get your hunting gear, you know, the case that is full of your arrows and that holds your bow? You will need them both, because I want you to go out and kill some wild animals for me to eat. I can taste it now!! Please cook it the way that you know I like it. Put some onions in there, thyme, ginger, red peppers, some vegetables and just season it up reeeaaalllllllyyy good!! Oh yeah, don't forget the curry! I am getting goose bumps just thinking about it."

Isaac continued, "Make some jasmine rice to go along with it and of course some good ole fashioned cast iron skillet corn bread. I heard that one of Cain's sons or grandson, one of them, came out with this new fancy cast iron skillet that has dividers, that way you won't need to slice it for me, you can just bring the entire skillet! So son, I am counting on you and need you to do that for me. Please make sure that you put it in a nice BIG bowl! After I eat I will give you my blessing before I die!"

Just as it is today with nosey people ear hustling our conversation, Rebekah was a master ear hustler and eaves dropped on the conversation that Isaac and Esau had! I am shaking my head because that's just shameful!

So, when Esau left to go hunting for the wild game for Isaac, Rebekah, with her scheming hustling self, ran to Jacob and said, "Hey, check this out. I overheard a conversation between your father and Esau."

Jacob looked at his mother with the side-eye and said, "YOU overheard?"

Rebekah said, "Ok, ok, I was ear hustling but, anywho, your father told your brother to go out and get some wild game, and begged him to PLEASE cook it the way that he likes it, so he can have some before he dies. Now listen up because I am going to give you the recipe of what he wants, he said 'put some onions in there, thyme, ginger, red peppers, some vegetables and just season it up really good and don't forget to add some curry. Make some jasmine rice to go along with it and of course some good ole fashioned cast iron skillet corn bread.'

Rebekah continued, "He wants it cooked in the new skillet, you know the one that you just bought from one of Cain's grandsons? Then take him a BIG bowl of it to eat and after he eats he will give Esau his blessing before he dies! So Jacob, I want you to have that blessing. I want you to make the stew according to the recipe that I just gave you and take the skillet of cornbread and the stew to your father and act like you are your brother Esau."

When Jacob heard this he was 38 hot because he was left out of the conversation that Isaac had with Esau. He was even more shocked that Esau had not told their father that he sold his birthright to him for a bowl of red stew! Isaac knew that Esau could not cook, that it was Jacob who cooked, so why didn't he include both of them and say, 'Esau get the wild game and Jacob cook it the way that I like?'

Jacob said to his mother, "How can I pretend to be Esau? Esau has hair all over, everywhere and well, me on the other hand, ya know I have that soft skin, baby soft smoooooth skin. Besides daddy knows us by our smells, since he can't see anymore, his nose has become like a hound dog. He can smell everything! Esau smells like the outdoors, just like those animals that he hunts and kills. And while we are on this topic, could you please talk to Esau about how he smells? It's just ratchet! I have tried to talk to him and I have even gone so far as to tell him that he smells funk horrible but he says he needs to blend in with the aroma of nature, so that he can hunt and the animals won't detect him. That is all well and good while he is hunting but when he comes home and sits at THIS table he needs to be funkless."

Jacob continued, "Back to the topic at hand, now mother you know that there is a big difference in how Esau smells and how I smell. I smell like food in the kitchen and after I cook I put on essential oils and what if daddy touches me? I don't want to trick my own father!! Wouldn't I curse myself by tricking him? If I am cursed my children will also be cursed!!"

Rebekah then said to him, "Chile, you worry too much! Don't worry about all of that nonsense! Since I am the one that came up with this idea and you are only being obedient to me your mother, let the curse fall on me. I am old anyways and don't have much time left here so, just do what I say; go and get the wild game and other ingredients and I will hook it up like your father wants it. What are you waiting for?! Go on now and you betta move like you gotta purpose! We both know that it doesn't take Esau that long to catch and kill a wild animal."

Once Jacob heard his mother say that the curse would fall on her, he bought it hook line and sinker! He went and got everything his mother needed to make the stew and she prepared it just like Isaac said he wanted it.

Now Rebekah was very crafty in her plot! While the stew was simmering she went to Esau's closet and took some of his clothes and made Jacob put the clothes on. She had not forgotten about how smooth Jacob's skin was versus how hairy Esau was so she covered Jacob's hands, arms and some of his neck with the goatskins. (GOAT SKIN, wow, Esau had to be very hair and the hair had to be course as a brush.) After she was pleased that this would work she gave Jacob the stew and cornbread to take to Isaac.

Jacob went to his father and said, "Hey daddy."

I would think that their voices should be different and that Isaac would know who it was from that, but Isaac answered, "Who is speaking to me right now? Is this my son Esau?"

Jacob said, "It's me, Esau. I did what you told me to do. It's time to sit up and dig into this food that you wanted. Some of my game and cornbread, cooked like you wanted. So please eat this so that you can bless me real good."

Isaac thought about it and said, "Wow that was awfully quick!! How did you hunt, kill the game, clean it, and cook it so quickly, my son? Did you even let it simmer so the meat would be tender and not tough?"

Jacob said, "For you daddy I hurried up, because you said you wanted it before you died and you didn't know how much longer you would be around, so the Lord helped me get it done quickly. You know how I do!"

Isaac thought to himself, Jacob really thinks that I have lost my mind, I may be blind, but I am not a fool. Isaac said, "Come a little closer!"

Isaac thought that if he came closer he would be able to touch him and from that he would know who he was talking to. Isaac knew that Esau was hairy like a goat and that Jacob had baby soft skin.

Jacob became very nervous then and thought to himself, "OH MY GOODNESS, he knows."

Jacob walked up to his father Isaac and Isaac touched him and said, "Your voice sounds like Jacob, but the skin on your hand feels like Esau."

Isaac did not recognize Jacob, because Jacob had goat skin on him that made his hands feel hairy like Esau's hands; so Isaac started to bless him, but before he did he asked one last time, "Esau, is this really Esau?"

Now this was Jacob's opportunity to come clean, but of course he did not, that lying spirit popped up an Jacob said, "Yes, daddy, I am really Esau."

Isaac was still skeptical, but thought about the food. There is a difference in the way that Jacob and Esau cook, so he said, "Well, okay, I am glad that it really is you, because I am starving and don't have time for any more games. Now bring me some of that good smelling food to eat, and then I will give you my blessing."

Jacob brought it to him and Isaac ate it all! The bowl and skillet were clean! Isaac also drank some wine with it. Then Isaac thought okay the food was off the chain, but I am still not convinced, plus I did not ask for wine. With my high blood pressure and sugar diabetes Esau knows that I don't drink wine. So Isaac said to Jacob, "Esau that was so good! All that I need now is a kiss from my son, who has honored me by hunting and cooking the food the way that I like it."

Isaac thought to himself, "If he kisses me I can get a good whiff of his body odor and touch his neck to see if he is hairy there also."

Even though Isaac knew how badly Esau smelled nobody beside Jacob would tell Esau that he was stink. He was such a big, strong man that most were scared of what he might do! No one in the family understood how Esau was able to get one wife let alone two wives! How did they get past the odor?!

So Jacob was nervous and sweating by now, but he did go over to his father and kiss him on the forehead. When Isaac caught the smell of his clothes, he thought to himself, "Well, ok, he passed all three tests. I guess this truly is Esau."

So Isaac blessed him and said, "Ah, this is my son Esau because you smell like the outdoors and wild animals."

Was this Isaac's way of politely telling his son Esau, 'Son, you stink?'

Isaac continued, "May God give you the morning dew by letting you have a long life and the richness of all things. I ask the Lord to give you an overload of grain and wine. May people of all nations serve you and bow at your presence. You will be over your brothers, and they will bow down to you. In closing remember those who come for you to do you harm will be cursed and those who stand by you in good times and bad will be blessed."

This happened with perfect timing because just as soon as Isaac got the last words of blessing out of his mouth and Jacob left to go back to his mother and report how things went, Esau pulled up from hunting. Esau went straight into the kitchen and he too prepared some tasty food and brought it to his father. Jacob was all over Esau's case about not washing up first and smelling up the kitchen. He said, "Boy you just nasty!"

Esau paid Jacob no attention, because he knew what he had to do to get his father's blessing, especially since he had sold his birthright to Jacob for a bowl of red stew. Esau rushed into to where Isaac was and said, "Okay father, I finally made it back and cooked the game and cornbread just as you said. I even used that new skillet, apparently Jacob had already bought one and it was freshly washed in the sink. So here ya go, please sit up and eat some of this delicious food that I have made just for YOU, just like you like it and then after you eat these tasty morsels you can give me your blessing like you said you would."

Isaac heard this and said, "Now what a minute, what is going on here and who in the world are you?"

Esau said, "You know who I am, have you forgotten me that quickly? I am Esau your oldest son!"

Isaac was PISSED at this point and was violently trembling because he had just given away Esau's blessing, but he did not know to whom he gave it. Isaac wanted to suddenly lay hands of another kind on somebody!

Isaac said, "If you are Esau, tell me who was it that just left out of here after I ate the freshly cooked game and cornbread and wine? Who was it! Who was it that brought all of that good food to me, just like I like it? I JUST ate and drank JUST before you came in and I blessed whoever that was and indeed the food was so good that he received a great blessing indeed! I should have known something was up, it felt very suspect. It really felt suspect because I did not say that I wanted wine with the meal. You would think that as old as I am, that I would know to follow my mind."

When Esau heard what his father said, he broke down into a gutter most cry! Ya know one of those loud, gritty and bitter cries, just hurt and angry at the same time! When he caught his breath from crying Esau begged his father to bless him too. He said "I have done what you asked me to do and you said that you would bless me, now please bless me too! I did not trick you or deceive you. I don't know who it was that ran game on you, I just know that it wasn't me. I did what you asked and I need my blessing!"

Isaac, put two and two together and figured that his ear hustling wife Rebekah and his youngest son Jacob ran game on him and he said to Esau, "It couldn't have been anyone but your mother and brother that did this! Who else is around here in ears distance that could have heard what I told you. MM Hmm, your mama is up to her old tricks again. She loves ear hustling, ya know that's her thing. So it was your brother who came up in here, ran game on me and stole your blessing like a thief in the night. Those two are out of control and always have been out of control."

Esau said, "But his name is Jacob which means to take advantage of, he is an opportunist! How could he do this to me and to YOU, his elderly blind father? You know that this is the SECOND time he has taken advantage of me! The first time I had been out in the fields all day and was hungry to the point that I felt like I was going to pass out, so I asked for some red stew and Jacob told me that the only way I could get some of the red stew was that I had to give him my birthright, my inheritance in exchange for some stew!! He stole my birthright, and now he's stolen my blessing! I am so sick of him stealing from me and acting like he is better than me because he works inside and I am in the fields!!"

Esau continued, "Father don't you have ANY kind of blessing that you can give me? You don't have any reserve blessings, like a private stash, for ME?"

Isaac answered Esau and said, "Son, I am so sorry. I have made Jacob to be your leader as well as to lead all of his relatives and his servants. I also have given him massive amounts of grain and new wine. I do not know what I have left for you? There is nothing left!"

Esau said to his father, "A man such as yourself, full of riches and bountifully blessed, why is it that you have only one blessing? After all of these years you should be able to bless me with at least something from your stash that the Lord gave you and maybe from what granddad Abraham left you!"

Esau was so broken up about this that he continued to cry. You know this was some kind of pain for a grown hairy man to cry like a baby.

Isaac felt so bad that he allowed this to happen to him, He also felt bad that he could not keep his word to his son Esau and bless him as he originally wanted to, so he said to Esau, "Esau, listen son, this is all that I can bless you with, you will no longer work in the fields and enjoy the outside. You will live like a warrior and you will work under your brother's authority. However, hold tight to these words, because when you finally grow tired of serving Jacob you will be able to break away from him and his power. Yes, you will be able to get out from under his control."

Esau took the blessing, but was not at all happy with what happened or the blessing his father gave him. Esau was out for Jacob's throat. The grudge was very intense because his brother Jacob had taken everything that was rightfully his. Esau didn't even know that he had caught the spirit of Cain (Cain killed Abel) because Esau said to himself, "I have had enough of Jacob! When the Lord calls my father Isaac home to be with Him, I'm gone kill Jacob! I will repay him for what he has done to me and take back what is rightfully mine! Jacob just has no idea that I am coming for him and with a vengeance!"

Rebekah had her servants listening out, because she knew that Esau had a temper. Anyone born with red hair all over their body and that stays in the fields with the animals not only has a temper but strength and strategy.

When Rebekah's servant told her what Esau said, right away she sent for her favorite son, Jacob. When Jacob arrived, he was like, "What is the big state of emergency around her mother. I was whipping up a new batch of lemon ginger chicken wings with golden mustard sauce. What is so important that it couldn't wait?"

Rebekah said, "Esau has found out what we did and he is coming for you. He found out how we plotted to steal his blessing from your father Isaac. He is 12 gauge hot and is planning to kill YOU!!"

Jacob interrupted and said, "He found out what WE plotted and did?! This was all your idea I was just being obedient to you. You said that the curse would be on you!

So if you are willing to take the curse, stand up to Esau and Father and own what you did! Now my brother wants to kill me because of your devious idea."

Rebekah said, "Now then, my son, calm down, you are such a pansy, that's why I had to coach you to do this in the beginning. Calm down and do what I say!"

Jacob said, "Oh you want me to be obedient to you again?! What will happen to me this time from following your plan?! I can only imagine what you have in mind!!"

Rebekah said, "BOY!! Look, we don't have time for this foolishness. So we got caught, now it is time for plan B. I need you to ride out, right now and go to my brother's crib in Harran. He is your uncle Laban. Once you are there do not tell him why you are just popping in and visiting out of nowhere, just say that you wanted to finally meet him. He will be kind and invite you in and when he does that is your opportunity to just stay there for a while until Esau calms down. Once Esau DOES calm down and forgets about what we did, I mean what you did to him, I'll send word for you that is safe for you to come back. I refuse to lose both of you."

Jacob said, "As stubborn as Esau is, I will be there for the rest of my life. Don't forget mother that Esau is a schemer just like you. He strategizes like a world champion chess player and like a general in the army. Can I at least go and see father one more time, we both know that he won't be around much longer?"

Rebekah said, "NO!! You must leave now. The servants have already packed your things and what you need to make the trip. Get your things and leave NOW. Your brother is on the war path."

Afterwards Rebekah went to see Isaac and said, "These Hittite women are just plain disgusting. They are definitely not what I want for Jacob. I know that Esau has married two of them and look at how much trouble and drama they cause around here. Now they have Esau wanting to kill Jacob. There is no one here for Jacob to take as a wife."

She continued, "The Hittite women are disgusting and If Jacob does takes a wife from among these women it will be chaos and I can't live with that!!"

Rebekah was such a drama queen and made it all about her. She continued to plot on behalf of Jacob and tried to play the innocent role with Isaac.

Will Isaac blast her for what she did and the confusion she caused?

Point to Ponder: Did Rebekah play right into the prophecy of Genesis 25? Did Isaac try to get around the word of the Lord with blessing Esau instead of Jacob? What did the Lord say to Rebekah in in Genesis 25 and would Esau not be as angry with his brother if he knew that this fulfilled prophecy?

Take Away: When situations arise in our lives and it seems that all is being taken away from us that we think and sometimes know that we rightfully deserve, look for the deeper reason of why and ask the Lord what can I do so that the intensity of the situation does not take me to a place that will cause me to say or do something that is way out of my character and that will cause further damage to my life. Be careful of the instructions that we follow, especially when we know that these instructions will deceive and harm others. Be so very careful to inventory our heart to seek out what lurks in the crevices and deep places.

Prayer: Father we thank You for revealing those things that are unseen in our life and for exposing hidden agendas that come to damage or destroy us and others connected to us. We thank You for the wisdom that You give us in all situations to overcome and remain victorious.

Genesis 28: PART ONE FINALE–Ear Hustler is at it AGAIN and Jacob eaves.

After Rebekah spoke those words to Isaac, Isaac began to think about what she said and did not want his wife to be miserable because of who his son Jacob marries. So Isaac sent a servant to get Jacob and once again Isaac blessed Jacob. This time the blessing came in the form of a command, because Isaac commanded Jacob by saying, "DO NOT marry a Canaanite/Hittite woman. DON'T YOU DO IT!! Leave here and leave with an urgency! Go to Paddan Aram which is your mother's hometown, Haran. This is where your mother's father Bethuel lives and look for your uncle Laban who has several daughters. I am sure that you will find a BAE there among your uncle's daughters. Choose one to be with. CHOOSE ONE! Don't be like your brother and have two wives. Now my son, may God bless you, and keep you. May He make you fruitful and increase you and your household to come. May you become a community of strong people. May God give you the same blessings that He gave to your grandfather Abraham and that is to allow you to take possession of the land where you will live as an outsider, which is the same land that God gave to your grandfather, Abraham."

After Isaac had blessed Jacob again, he sent Jacob on his happy go BLESSED, merry way. So Jacob left his father and mother and went to Paddan Aram, to see his Uncle Laban, the brother of his mother Rebekah.

Everything seemed to be going as Rebekah planned, right on schedule and peaceful, at least that was until Esau found out!! When Esau finally heard about what had taken place with Isaac and Jacob and how Jacob had once again been blessed by their father Isaac, HE WAS LIVID! BUT when he heard about how Isaac commanded Jacob NOT to marry a Canaanite/Hittite woman Esau REALLY got in his feelings and thought to himself that his father was doing way too much!

Esau was really beside himself. Esau thought that Isaac favored Jacob over him, when he and his father had always been so tight. Esau would have expected this from his mother Rebekah, because she was so close to Jacob, but the blow was super hard when Isaac blessed Jacob twice and without Esau being there. It was as if all of this was done behind his back. Esau began to realize that his father saw the Canaanite women as unworthy of being with Jacob, but not Esau. Esau said to himself, "Why does he care so much about who Jacob marries and never once has he said anything to me."

To spite his father Isaac, Esau went to Ishmael (son of Abraham) and married Mahalath, Ishamael's daughter and she was also the sister of Nebaioth. This marriage was done out of spite and it was also in addition to all of the other wives that Esau already had. Esau thought to himself, "Why is Jacob so special and why is so he blessed to go away to get a wife and I am left here to choose from what my father considers to be not good enough and the women that my mother calls disgusting? At least with him gone I do not have to serve under him!! I guess my father's little counterfeit blessing to me is slayed by his own words! Haha, hehe, I got the victory!!"

Jacob being the obedient son, did just as his father and mother had told him to, and that was to leave Beersheba and set out for Harran. Now because Jacob left so late in the day he didn't get to travel very far due to the sun setting and night falling, so he pulled over and stopped for the night. Jacob took one of the stones that was on the ground and put it under his head to use as a pillow to sleep. Can you imagine using a STONE as a pillow? Didn't the servants think to pack something for him to sleep on?

Nevertheless and anyways, once Jacob fell asleep he began to dream in 4K HD living color! He had a dream that he saw a stairway and the bottom of the stairway was on the earth, and the top of the stairway was reaching into heaven. WOW! Jacob also saw the angels of God going up and down the ladder.

When he looked further he could see the Lord standing there in heaven above the earth and the Lord said, "I am the LORD, the God of Abraham and of Isaac. I will give you and your family line the land on which you are resting. Your family will be so plentiful that they will be like the dust of the earth, and will be on the western, eastern, northern and southern parts of the earth. Everyone that crosses their path and those that do not come in their paths will be blessed because of you and your family. I will always be with you and I will be there looking out for you wherever you go. You will come back to this very land and I want you to always remember that I will not leave you until I have done what I have promised you."

When Jacob woke up from the dream, he thought to himself, "What a powerful dream. The Lord spoke to me exactly the words my father Isaac said, the blessing of Abraham!!"

Jacob then shouted out loud in a praise of joy saying, "Surely the LORD God is in THIS place!! I did not know this before I went to sleep, but best believe I know it now!!"

After Jacob thought about that, I mean he really thought about it, he became scared, but it was a good scared because he said out loud, "My, my, my how powerful is this spot! This cannot be anything other than the place where God lives; this IS the entry way to heaven."

Jacob did not want to leave this place, but he had to because he was being obedient to his mother and father and wanted to find a BAE. Early the next morning Jacob took the stone that he had used as a pillow and just like his father and grandfather, Jacob made an altar to the Lord. He anointed the altar with oil, by pouring oil on top of it. Jacob then thought that he should give it a name, so he named that place Bethel, which means house of God. He renamed the place to Bethel even though the city was named Luz.

After Jacob renamed the place, he made a vow unto the Lord and said, "Since the Lord God has promised to be with me, to watch over me on this journey, to give me all that I need and to allow me to one day go back to my hometown, then there is no reason on this earth why I can't make the Lord MY God!! I make the LORD MY God this day!! This altar that I have made will BE the house of God! And I vow that of all that I make financially and otherwise I will give the Lord my God ten percent."

Points to Ponder: Why did Isaac find it necessary to bless Jacob again? Was it because Jacob was leaving from under his protection? Is this something that we should do when our children leave the house for the day to go to school or to go off to college or as they leave to start their own lives and find their own path? Shouldn't we bless them as Isaac did Jacob?

Take away: Just as Jacob found joy in his dream as he went on his way, let us look at each day through the filter of joy and thanksgiving.

Prayer: Father we thank You today for changing the lens of our eyesight to that of joy and thanksgiving. Even though we may have to leave our place of comfort and familiarity we know that You are with us, that You will provide for us and that You will keep us safe in all that we set out to do. We ask for dreams and visions that will give joy, encouragement and direction. We declare this day that You are our God!

Stay tuned for part two of Genesis and find out more about Jacob's journey. Is his uncle Laban a scheming ear hustler like his mama? Will he find his one and only BAE? Oh yeah it gets even better!